A Supernatural Tour of the Great Lakes

Gone Missing!

Dennis Boyer

Badger Books Inc.
Oregon, WI

ISBN 1-878569-89-9

Badger Books Inc.
P.O. Box 192
Oregon, WI 53575
Toll-free phone: (800) 928-2372
Fax: (608) 835-3638
Email: books@badgerbooks.com
Web site: www.badgerbooks.com

In Memory of
Walt Bresette, a Red Cliff warrior of the waters,
Arthur "Tiny" Wells, a Manitowoc shipbuilder,
and the crew of the Linda E.

Contents

Acknowledgments

The landlubber owes a debt to many who have shared stories of time spent on the waters of the world. Among my earliest memories are the recollections of maternal uncles Sonny, Russ, Norm, and Dick from their service in the Navy and Coast Guard. My own military time, though more connected to air and ground operations, brought me to Vung Tau, Vietnam and a variety of U.S. and Australian naval personnel. Later I had the opportunity to spend time in the Pacific ports of Mexico and Central America and meet individuals on round the world trips and some permanently thrown ashore. I hoist and quaff a beer to memory of all of you.

More to the point are the people encountered in my favorite Great Lakes haunts. Much of this collection gestated during twenty years of trips to Red Cliff Reservation in Wisconsin, especially through contact with the Bresette, Gokee, and Peterson families. Add to that time spent at Bad River Reservation and my favorite taverns of Bayfield and Madeline Island. Throw in friendly staff at the Manitowoc Maritime Museum, Old Fort William in Thunder Bay, the Indiana Dunes, and the McKinley Marina in Milwaukee. And buy a round in my name (but not on my tab) at Nelsen's Hall on Washington Island.

Special thanks to those who aided or encouraged this effort to look at the stories of the three Big Sisters of Superior, Huron, and Michigan: Owen Coyle, Len Gundersen, Rob Olson, Susan Lampert Smith, Frank Koehn, Mary Stevenson, Rob Kruszynski, Dean Connors, Rick Murphy, Kevin Traas, Jennifer Grondin, Howard Schmidt, Johanna Knowles, Dave Henke, and Phil Neuenfeldt. And to Marv Balousek for making it happen.

Introduction

Gone Missing is my third collection of ghost stories and fifth collection of regional lore. It represents the biggest challenge I have confronted thus far in compiling accounts and organizing them in a way that would make some sort of sense. Readers of my other works are aware of my inclination to organize material bioregionally where possible. The material assembled here is presented in a slightly different form, that of legs of a journey constituting a circumnavigation of the Upper Great Lakes.

Some readers might wonder what happened to poor Erie and lonely Ontario in this endeavor. Naturally it occurred to me to include the lower two lakes. This was my most difficult compilation to date and it took far longer to assemble its material than for any of my prior works. There are, to be sure, strange accounts aplenty involving Lake Erie and Lake Ontario. In the end my personal contacts and knowledge of local context was too thin to put those lakes on equal footing with Michigan, Huron, and Superior.

Readers will also note that I use the term "the Big Sisters" interchangeably with Upper Great Lakes. It is not a term of my own coinage, rather representing a story artifact I acquired from members of the Lake Superior Ojibwe. I heard the words often enough in varied oral traditions that they took on a comfortable ring. Perhaps some day I will retell those stories.

Finally, I call attention to the legs of this circumnavigation and how the narratives shift in content and mood from shore to shore. There might not be anything approaching, let us say, an archetypal eastern Lake Michigan story. But I had the clear impression that the ethnic histories and settlement patterns on each shoreline made an impact on the way local residents tell and interpret accounts of hauntings and oddities.

As usual, I avoid probing evaluation of these accounts in ways that call the sources into question. If I have learned anything in my years of dealing with ghost stories, it is that the sources, if left to tell their stories unimpeded, can prove as interesting as the accounts they relate. I know they gave me the gift of seeing these large bodies of water in an entirely new light. I hope that this light shines through for those who peruse these pages.

Happy Sails to you,
Dennis Boyer

Part I
Up Lake Passage
on Michigan

Lost Flight

Great Lakes stories have always tugged at some part of me, especially those of the "Big Sisters" of Huron, Michigan, and Superior. Decades of wandering in the region, collecting its stories and studying its folklore, put a notion in my mind to someday compile a book of supernatural tales of the Great Lakes. Plenty of such concepts percolate in my writer's head, and from time to time the fates place opportunity in my path and books occasionally materialize. Often it takes a catalyst or an oracle, some circumstance or some source which grants me the gift of an individual narrative and inspires a voice or tone for an entire collection.

Edwin was the inspiration for this collection. He was exactly what one might have expected of a source of Great Lakes tales: a weekend sailor, former Navy man, and son and grandson of Norwegian merchant seamen. But that's where expectations ended. You'd think you'd run into a source like Edwin in a bar near a wharf or in a sleepy boat yard. You'd think that he'd be grouchy and unkempt. Instead Edwin gifted his story and his perspective to me during a long night's wait in the O'Hare terminal before a flight to Mexico. He was a pleasant and well groomed man of nearly 80, golden tan and bright blue eyes suggesting sturdy genes.

He approached me at one of the aviation displays that dot the terminal. This one was about World War II aircraft and naval aviation of that period. At first he spoke as people usually do when making conversation with strangers. But there was something about the jut of his chin that bespoke a connection to this subject matter. It wasn't a stretch to guess that a story would be forthcoming. It was where the story went that was unexpected.

*   *   *

Bet you didn't know that Chicago was one of the main spots for naval aviation training in those days. Everybody's heard of the Great Lakes Naval Training Center, but few know that it was a mainstay for aircraft carrier training in World War II. That's right, "flat top" flyers right here on Lake Michigan.

Remember, in the opening days of World War II the German U-boats were sinking U.S. shipping all along the Atlantic and Gulf coasts and the Japanese had the Pacific Coast in a near panic. That's why so much defense preparation and training was moved to the middle of the country. Invasion wasn't a real threat, but Pearl Harbor showed what could happen to poorly defended port facilities. That's the origin of many of the naval air stations away from the sea.

Of course there were no real aircraft carriers on the Great Lakes, there was no St. Lawrence Seaway to accommodate even the small carriers. We had training carriers here, cobbled together vessels of bastard origins. I think the one we used early on was an old ore boat. There may have been a later one that was a car ferry or some type of freighter. I was long gone by then.

Machinists, ironworkers, and welders refitted things like this in record time. No small thing in those times. Skilled shipworkers were in demand. Many went up-lake to Manitowoc, Wisconsin, where they built submarines. Metalworkers were busy at the works in East Chicago and Gary. Materials were in short supply, shipments erratic, and savvy quartermasters were stealing everything that wasn't bolted down and sometimes torched the bolts and made off with that stuff, too.

The training flat top was not a pretty sight, a bit ungainly with its flight deck that looked like a butcher block on a row boat. But it served its purpose. It had some chief petty officers you'd swear had been at Manila Bay with Dewey in '98. The center turned out some naval aviators who flew with the best of them in every fleet theater that floated aircraft carriers. More than a few of those boys didn't come back.

But look at this airport exhibit and you'll figure out that even training takes its toll. We had a flight that simply disappeared over Lake Michigan. It was assumed that they ran out of fuel and went down in the lake. This was different than crashes on takeoff or landing, which are a price of business on carriers. It was also different than severe weather losses. Here it was limited visibility and nothing more.

So was it a matter of disorientation and poor navigation? You get turned the wrong way out on that lake, set a wrong heading and you can fly a long way north and never see land, especially if the fog has its padlocks on the hatches from Indiana Dunes to

Ludington to Green Bay. In those conditions you could even over-shoot the Upper Peninsula and come down in Ontario. But with the fuel amounts in those trainers it's more likely that they went down somewhere out in that long stretch up the middle of the lake.

Still, it could have been something else. A shift in magnetism. A freak storm out on the lake. A series of flying misjudgments caus-ing a multi-aircraft collision. Or some Great Lakes version of the Bermuda Triangle.

Naval aviation has such accidents and will always have them as long as men insist on taking off from pitching platforms day and night in weather foul or fair. But the Great Lakes, especially beau-tiful Lake Michigan, seem less a scene for such loss. The long blue gal is deceptive that way, her sparkly smile and smooth complexion can lull you into moon-eyed marvel. It can be very jarring when such a beauty turns on you and you feel the sting of her slap on your face. She can be fickle and demanding, yes she can.

Forty years of sailing on these big lakes and flying over them has taught me a few things. Like a marriage, you have to make adjust-ments if you want to survive. Like a marriage, some things are better left unsaid or forgiven and forgotten. Yet I can't forget that Lost Flight, the damn lake won't let me.

On my very last training flight over the lake I thought I saw them, though they had disappeared weeks earlier. Again, on a plea-sure trip with the family in my first four seater in the 1950s, I thought I saw them disappear into a large bank of cumulus. About ten years later, on our second sailboat, I heard those old trainer engines sput-ter and fail in a fog bank east of Racine. Then I saw them from the airline's corporate jet just before I retired. They looked like they were circling in a pattern like we did when we couldn't get a bear-ing on the ship.

There are others who've seen the Lost Flight, others who had some connection to that time and those circumstances. Most of them are former aviators who trained with those fellows and who also know a thing or two about the lake. Most have lived long full lives, have seen the world, and have their share of stark memories from the carrier air battles in the Pacific. Many lost friends under brutal circumstances.

The Lost Flight doesn't stick with us just because of loss of life. We saw plenty of that. It was the loss of innocence that hit us long before we heard a shot fired. It was a matter of expectation and surprise. We thought we were immortal, too jaunty and dashing to die. We didn't yet know that the Grim Reaper reaches out to tap on the shoulder without regard for your personal plans. We didn't yet know that this old globe is a big place, with plenty of waters, jungle, deserts, and mountains of scale beyond human comprehension that can swallow you up.

It's this tone of mystery of things beneath the surface that connects me to the Lost Flight and those big lakes. There are deep forces at work out there, with all the raw power of water space. Large bodies of water do indeed just swallow things up. Sometimes they even send their mists and their storms ashore to do their work beyond the reach of waves. Old mariners say that each of the big lakes has a big spirit that is kept company by the spirits or souls claimed by the waters.

That's the fate of the Lost Flight, to be part of the entourage of the Michigan Manitou. Maybe that's the place those of us with lake and aviation connections will go. You think that might be it? I've wondered about that ever since that day when a trip to the dispensary kept me from being on the Lost Flight.

Cholera Canal

L ake lore tends to focus on history and nature's power and beauty. When an old tale raises questions about man's folly on the lakes it tends to zero in on issues of imprudent seamanship. Only in more recent times has deeper understanding of public health and ecology generated appreciation about the impact of industrialization on the Great Lakes.

In many ways it was Lake Michigan that first felt the brunt of man's heavy steel hand. Not that Ontario and Erie were left unmolested; their earlier settlement by Europeans left the little sisters of the east violated by the time of the War of 1812. But it was Lake Michigan that first felt the full forces of that breed of man who consciously sought to subdue nature and bend it to his own purpose. Such men were, in their own day, acclaimed as forward thinking pioneers. Those who questioned the march of progress were derided as crackpots.

The referral that brought me to Lake Calumet Harbor made no reference to such matters. It was only to ask for Norton, an office manager in one of the port facility offices. He was reputed to know where the bodies were buried in Lake Michigan, both metaphorically and literally. He was indeed a font of knowledge about eerie things from Gary to Point aux Chenes. But his very first account was perhaps the most haunting.

*   *   *

Before ship traffic was re-geared to oceangoing vessels, the main cargo facilities were on the Chicago River. There's a seamy side to how shipping got built up in the area and how they played God with the waters to make it happen. All the massive navigation projects have taken a toll, from the St. Lawrence Seaway and Sag Channel of modern times, back to the Sanitary and Ship Canal. But the real impact on people and nature came earlier, back in the 1940s with the Illinois and Michigan Canal.

Maybe you can blame the whole thing on Louis Jolliet. In the 1670s the French explorer pontificated on the wonders of a Lake Michigan-Mississippi River connection. But, heck, that was Jules

Verne stuff back in that era. Then in 1827 someone in the U.S. government dusted off those old fantasies and Congress issued a 300,000 acre land grant to finance a canal.

Neither Jolliet nor the federal bureaucrats were qualified geologists. The work proved daunting given the level of technology available in those days. It's one thing to dig a few miles of drainage ditch through farm country loam. But it's quite another thing to push almost a hundred miles through clay and rock. That's why efforts to start sputtered until 1836 and then took twelve years to bring to completion.

Not a thought was given to the environmental implications of what they had wrought, connecting one great body of water with another. It was the harbinger of things to come, like lampreys and zebra mussels. But the short term consequences were actually pretty dramatic, too, though rationalized and misunderstood. The artificial body of water soon became a source of disease.

As strange as it sounds, early Chicagoans thought the canal a fine place to dump their growing volume of sewage. Most civil engineers would tell you, aesthetics and hygiene aside, that a canal system with locks is not the best system to carry waste away from you. There's just not enough pull in such a system. What you end up with, as they did with the Illinois and Michigan Canal, is a virtually stagnant system with your effluent pulled into your backwaters.

In this case those backwaters were the Des Plaines and upper Illinois rivers. Those bodies of water, the Chicago River, the old harbor, and the canal itself were all turned into open sewers. Various schemes to relieve the clogged waterways simply spread the filth, sometimes backflushing it into Lake Michigan itself. It gave a squalid air to the whole waterfront. Sailors' songs contain accounts describing the old port of Chicago waters in words usually reserved for the dankest harbors of Asia.

Still, it wasn't just aromas that made for unpleasantness. By the eve of the Civil War there had been sickness associated with the water contamination. Mostly smaller outbreaks at first. Then some contagion that moved through little communities associated with the waterfront. Entire immigrant families were wiped out. The worst incident was supposed to be cholera in the early 1860s. It moved through the Irish shanties and Black shacks. Many victims of the disease, too poor for burial, were thrown into the canal under cover of darkness. It was said that heavy storms caused some bodies to be pulled out of the port and into the lake.

This is where legend gets thrown in with history. It was said that crews of the barges and light steamboats that plied the canal would turn back if they encountered a flotilla of corpses in what they called the "cholera canal." Likewise for vessels entering the old port of Chicago. It was an ill omen for lake sailors should the Chicago River be discharging corpses into the lake. In such conditions captains dropped anchor and waited for a different wind.

The odd thing is that the corpses were seen long after nature's decay would have claimed them or recycled them as it were. So various stories about rude spirits started to circulate among lake men. Some ascribed the hauntings to the corruption and greed behind the canal's construction, ever the foundation of any Chicago public works project. Some harkened back to an alleged Potawatomi curse issued in retribution for the European gift of the smallpox epidemic that emptied the once numerous lodges of that tribe. A few who knew of the French Jesuit mission that stood at the mouth of the Chicago River say that the militant priests were among the first claimed by disease and thrown into the waters. Others say that the trigger was disease in the U.S. outpost of Fort Dearborn, at the corner of the present-day Wacker Drive and Michigan Avenue, which encouraged the local Indians to slaughter the occupants and burn the fort in the War of 1812.

Whatever the unholy chain of events, it is clear that something is out of balance. We modern people think that we fully understand the disease paradigm, that it's all a matter of infectious agents, inoculation, and antibiotics. We laugh at primitive peoples who attribute disease to spirits. But what of the imbalance in our current way of life that impairs the spirit? What of the toxins and stresses that impair the immune system? What mechanisms might a large ecosystem like Lake Michigan have to defend itself against the human organism? Not hard to imagine how we'd get ourselves jammed up by our behavior if you even believe a tenth of the implications of the Earth as an integrated and responsive, maybe even conscious, system.

I've got many of Chicago's bloodlines in me: African, Irish, Polish, and Italian. Granny Dubois claimed Jean Baptiste Du Sable and Miami Indians as ancestors. All were viewed as expendable people at one time or another. Here I am, a descendant, with a decent job and a twenty-four foot watercraft. Still, I see those floaters from the old Cholera Canal when I come back in late.

It's those late July and early August nights — times of swelter-ing temperatures, high humidity, and wind out of the southwest. The breeze brings a stink off the city and up out of the canal. In that dim light of faded dusk there's often a moment when I see the bodies for an instant, then they're gone. My friend Murphy has seen them, too, from his lake rig. It's not just me; I've met others who worked the old harbor who've seen the ghostly bodies.

Sometimes when the water is particularly brackish the heads of corpses seem to bob upright. They don't talk of course. But their faces seem to say something. There's a look of pleading not to be forgotten. But there's also a look of warning in the glimpses I catch of those faces. It's a message of unfinished business between the lake and those who toy with it.

Ghosts of Petite Fort

Historical reenactors are generally good sources for yarns. They know not only the details of material life in their periods of interest, but also strive mightily to capture the spirit of those times. Whether they do so with fidelity to facts is a bone of contention between reenactors and academic historians. Reenactors are not bashful about incorporating the earthy folkways of our pioneer ancestors into their repertoire. This "warts and all" approach leaves the more delicate souls of local historical societies gasping for air at times.

Reenactors also have their run-ins with bureaucrats as they struggle for secure access to sites that relate to themes of interest. One would like to think that those charged with the administration of public lands might like the support of a robust and interested constituency. But that is often not the case with public servants conditioned to turf wars and rigid application of regulations. There is often elevated official regard for the bricks and mortar of historic or scenic sites and official neglect of the folkloric content of that same property. It often happens that public property managers strive to suppress stories of haunting at the parks and facilities under their supervision.

That's what Carl thinks is happening at Indiana Dunes State Park. He is setting up a camp with other reenactors just off U.S. Highway 12 and Indiana Highway 49. The burly facsimile of an 18th Century voyageur is only too glad to take a break from the labor of setting up camp and share a cold fermented beverage.

*   *   *

People don't know what they have in their backyard, be it history or hauntings. People just think of the dunes here and don't realize what went on here. They don't realize there were battles fought here. Battles fought between French and British after the first round of fur wars. Fighting all the way up through the American Revolution, long after France had lost New France in Canada.

The first stockade was built as more of a trading post, thus the name Petite Fort. It turned out to be a good observation post, with commanding views from nearby dunes. Fort Creek at that time had a spring credited with healing powers. Other spiritual significance was attached to the dunes themselves by the original inhabitants.

The first fight here took place between tribes allied with the French and those allied with the English in the 1740s. A little later the French built the stockade to protect the fur trade. In the 1750s and 1760s the fort took on significance in the last stage of the French and Indian Wars. It was a staging point for the Indian allies of the French, for their raids east to the English colonies. Even after the French lost that war there were French traders operating out of the fort, staying on at the sufferance of the English. Of course, the American Revolution brought more tension to the old frontier, and the British formally took over the fort at one point only to abandon it. Then toward the end of the Revolution, pro-American French partisans used the fort as a base in the raid against the British at Fort St. Joseph up in Michigan. A counterattack resulted in a battle right here in the dunes.

This is what the ghosts in the dunes stem from. Yeah, ghosts right around old Petite Fort and the Fort River. Not that the park people at Indiana Dunes or at the National Lakeshore want to hear about it. There was one naturalist at the park who was interested in the ghosts, but the higher-ups put the lid on it. I guess hauntings aren't considered part of park authorized activities.

We've seen the ghosts. They're quite striking, with sashes and feathered clubs. There are Indians with painted faces, French officers and voyageur irregulars, British troops, and colonial militia scouts. You can see them in the brush on moonlit nights. An old-timer from a dunes homesteading family said that these spirits are locked in an eternal battle for the fort. He told me years ago that those ghosts refight the battles whenever there is an important celestial event, things like eclipses or full moons on solstices. I saw the war parties come in by canoe in the moonlight of an autumnal equinox almost twelve years ago.

At first I thought they were reenactors and I said to myself, "This is really cool." But I soon realized that there just aren't that many reenactors portraying Indians. These rascals came in dozens and dozens of canoes. I also realized that most reenactors have little skill for stealth. The group I watched moved silently except for the muffled sound of the paddles on the lake. Then, right as they were about to land on the shore, they disappeared into a mist!

You hear bits and pieces of legends of why this phenomenon might occur here at the dunes. You can find dozens of people who say they met an old Indian man in the dunes who told them that this is a powerful place from a spirit angle. It's fairly well known in reenactor circles that modern day Native American medicine men often travel to sacred sites that are located in their original home territory. That's what I thought people were running into here. But last year I had an encounter that made me reassess that angle.

I ran into an old fellow right up the trail here shortly before dusk. He looked absolutely sun-baked, so wrinkled that I couldn't tell if he was 60 or 106. We talked awhile about this and that and I asked him where he was from. He said he was from right here. I asked him if he was pulling my chain. He just smiled and pointed over my shoulder, behind me. I turned and there was an eagle or osprey circling above, something we don't see that often here. I admired it for a bit and then turned back to him and he was gone! Then I turned back to the bird and it was gone! I whipped around again to see if I could catch a glimpse of him going down the trail or see a track in the sand. Nothing! But looking down I noticed a big old turtle, not a snapper, crawling away in the weeds. What do you make of that?

What I make of it is that there is a strong presence here, something that was disturbed by those fur wars. Maybe something that is older than the tribes who were here. Maybe something as old as the lake itself. Some power that accumulated here along with the sand, something that winds and waves pushed here. That would account for the stories of storms that came up suddenly and sank war parties and traders right off Fort Creek.

I should mention that when people see these ghosts it's often in the low spots in the sand known as blowouts or sand bowls. These are places where channeled wind has carved out a circular depression, sometimes just about perfect. And sometimes there'll be a faint design in these blowouts, like a sand painting in a spiral that works to a dark spot in the center. It's hard to believe nature can do such a thing on its own, but I suppose it's possible that rotating wind can sift out and drop sand and debris based on size and weight. Yet when you look at one of those spirals, it draws you in, like there was some deeper meaning to it.

If ghosts are seen it's often when a dust devil or whirlwind has kicked up loose matter in one of these blowouts. When the apparitions disappear there's often a second whirlwind. So it must have something to do with the power of the elements, the wind and the lake. Maybe even the sun, there are pockets of heat around here, even in cool weather.

Oh, I forgot to mention what happened the day after I saw the old man last year. It was summer solstice, a hot one. I got up early to walk down to the beach. The air felt strange, like before a thunderstorm, but there wasn't a cloud in the sky. The peaks of Mt. Tim, Mt. Jackson, and Mt. Holden, the three big dunes, were already in bright sunlight. As the sun chased the shadows off the beach and out of the blowouts I saw dust rise up to the east. When it got closer I could see it was a squad of dust devils. The small ones dissipated and one remaining large one seemed to climb Mt. Jackson. It ended in a puff of sand sparkling in the sunlight. When the dust settled, the old man was standing on top of Mr. Jackson, looking out at the lake.

So that's why I'm here one year later. I want to see if he shows up tomorrow.

Lady of the Lighthouse

J ourneys around the Big Sisters of Michigan, Huron, and Superior made me suspect that almost every lighthouse has a ghost story or two. The often lonely spots, some quite isolated, were fertile ground for tragic circumstances and exposure to raw elements. Even the port town lighthouses were set apart from community life a bit, sometimes with access only by pier, jetty, catwalk, or dingy. Even one on the mainland proper could be cut off by storms or ice windrows.

Lighthouse fans on the lakes would also fill me with stories of eccentric hermits who tended lighthouses. Such tales often had the air of the disreputable about them, making reference to excessive drinking, madness, and strange goings on. More than a few lighthouse keepers met untimely ends. Of those unfortunate lake servants a goodly number hang on in spirit form in the environs of their former residences. Informants also took pains to relate the isolation and tedium of the trade of lighthouse keeper.

Not so with Wilma. When I first spoke to her by phone she was bubbling with the poetry of lighthouse life. She thought every lighthouse a potential Walden Pond for a budding Thoreau. She herself had acted as a volunteer resident at several national lakeshore lighthouses. Her lighthouse stories were brimming with talk of family life, robust children, and the lessons of nature. She made me aware of the role of women in the lighthouses of the Upper Great Lakes.

Eventually I managed to visit her at her home in Michigan City, Indiana. She struck me as a typical grandmotherly type, showing a preference for jeans and flannel not common among women who grew up in the Depression. During my visit she managed to surprise me with a private tour of the Old Lighthouse at Michigan Park. But she surprised me even more with this heretofore unhinted at tale.

*   *   *

A lady's spirit still inhabits this lighthouse, you know? Yes, yes, she's been seen here since the early 1900s. She was the lighthouse keeper for over half a century, from 1858 to 1904. She was light-house tender of another lighthouse at least as early as 1853. Her name was Harriet Colfax, but many of us call her the Lady of the Lighthouse.

Michigan City was planned in different way from most ports, the others being as much a product of accident as design. But the Indiana legislature actually caused Michigan City by a law which provided for a road to run across the length of the state, from the Ohio River to Lake Michigan. Michigan City is where that road met the lake. It was that legislative act that caused Harriet Colfax and nearly a thousand other people to flock to the site before the road was even completed.

The road was indeed advantageous to Michigan City. The farm boom in the area meant a brisk trade in shipping grain right from the outset. Not far behind was a growing commercial fishery that was soon shipping fresh, smoked, and dried fish. By the 1850s the shipping trade out of Michigan City was also handling a large volume of hogs and cattle. The railroads reached Michigan City, both the Michigan Central and the Monon, and the town became a crossroads of commerce. By the beginning of the Civil War we had Germans, Swedes, and Norwegians working in mills, foundries, and railroad car shops. We had one of the most improved harbors outside the eastern states. And that meant a lighthouse.

The first lighthouse was a rough affair, supposedly a stone tower without a house. Then came a temporary frame building that lasted until 1858. Harriet worked the last five years of that lighthouse. Then the federal government built this basic structure. Harriet worked this one for almost another fifty years. After she was gone the government remodeled it in 1904 and eventually put electricity in it. But the flavor of the place is still hers and her presence is strong.

Harriet was kind of a patron saint to many of the lake boatmen and fishing families. She lived frugally and modestly like they did. She was well thought of by the old New Englanders and the Scandinavians, no small trick in a town that had some noticeable ethnic divisions in those days. There were some family connections, too, and some sad personal history, but I'll leave that to others to dig around in.

I prefer to think of her as a strong independent woman, a woman ahead of her time. Oh, I know, a fair number of women tended lighthouses. And it often was the result of death or disability of the father or husband, and the jobs were more or less inherited. But most of that happened at remote lighthouses, islands cut off by ice and storms five months of the year. Harriet, on the other hand, held the job in brawny male-dominated town with a large labor force.

Who knows if all the stories about her are true? Some, maybe most, have the ring of truth to them. For instance, the claim that she rang a bell by hand straight through a night of deathly fog when there were overdue sailing ships still out. Or that she kept watch with a spyglass when fishing boats were reported lost. Or when she spotted a capsized lake schooner in the early dawn and sent a rescue party. The stories themselves suggest how deeply embedded she was in the hearts of those connected to the lake.

Perhaps that's why some of us continue to see her. Maybe she's stuck in the community's consciousness. I've heard of ghosts who are troubled and can't let go of this earthly plane. Does the reverse ever occur? Where a ghost is held fast to a place by the memories the living hold onto? Even three or four generations later, after all those with actual knowledge are gone?

It was my Aunt Martha who told me about the Lady of the Lighthouse. As a young girl I sought to see her, but never did. Aunt Martha actually knew Harriet while alive and had tea with her here in the lighthouse. At a tender age I fancied the idea of having tea with the Lady of the Lighthouse ghost, but the keeper of that time was fairly gruff and not partial to visitors.

I did not see the Lady of the Lighthouse until after the Coast Guard shut down the facility in 1960. Automated lights and beacons made these old lighthouses obsolete. The thought of this closure must have made the lady more determined than ever to keep her vigil. I believe it was in 1961 that I first saw a figure up in the lantern room. I saw her almost every summer after that.

What was unusual was that I saw her as a younger woman and in a white dress. I know that's consistent with a summer theme and the fashion of her era. But she was a working woman and not within the fashion orbit of the ladies who summered in cottages near the lake. When I talked about that with the historically inclined who run the lighthouse as a museum these days, they didn't think the circumstances fit. The photos of Harriet show her modestly and simply attired in dark clothes.

Later I was vindicated a bit when an estate sale at one of the old mansions turned up a photo of a young Harriet in a white dress.

But the solution to the one set of questions spawned a new series of questions. Why did a well-off family keep a photo of a poor light-house keeper? Was there a connection between someone in that family and Harriet? What feminine hand inscribed Harriet's name on that photo in firm cursive and boldly underlined it? Was the inscription's emphasis a matter of affection, disdain, or jealousy? Might not that dress have come from the same house as the photo?

It's an interesting mystery. Probably one without solution. But the answer might put a whole new light on why the Lady of the Lighthouse watches the lake so intently.

The Phantom Chicora

A	Great Lakes circumnavigation can turn up many a tale of ghost ships. Michigan, Huron, and Superior are among the most storm-lashed bodies of inland waters in the world and have claimed more than their share of vessels from paleo-Indian animal hide boats to modern great steel behemoths. In many cases, details of these maritime species are sparse and vague.

When ghost ships are seen it is usually a fleeting observation. They are the stuff of near collisions in banks of fog, the looming presences in the dark night passages, and the spume-obscured glimpses in horrific storms. The observers often have a physical response to those sightings, a visceral reaction that informs instinct that their experience was indeed unworldly and not the product of optical allusion or overactive imagination. Ghost ship sightings are often a once in a lifetime occurrence for the observer.

Joe's experience was quite different, and his relationship to the subject matter was not casual. When I caught up to him he was mowing the grass across the way from the Morton House museum on Territorial Road in Benton Harbor, Michigan. At first he seemed like a reluctant source and insisted on finishing the lawn. It turned out that he was simply an orderly man with a quiet sharing side. He sat in the grass to have his lunch, offered half a sandwich and a whole story.

*   *   *

It feels a little odd, telling this story on a day so beautiful that you could just about see across Lake Michigan from a high tree. You see, the *Chicora* was lost in a terrible winter storm over a hundred years ago. It's always winter when I see its phantom.

You'll have to ask others about what they see. There are plenty of fishermen who see phantom ships out in the lake at all times of the year. They see all sorts of craft in all sorts of conditions. Do any of them see the *Chicora*? That's something I can't really answer. Some say they do. But if you talk to any of them, be sure to ask them to describe the ship. It's quite distinctive, a very long package steamer with a forward wheelhouse, white on the upper deck, and single stack amidships.

The ship had a distinguished twelve year history of shipping before she was lost. She was built in 1882 for the combined trade of passengers and freight. In her day she was just about the classiest vessel on the lakes. The cabins came close to the luxury of the oceanliners, with tropical wood paneling and fine furnishings. While a wooden ship in basic construction, it had the look of the later steel ships. It was over 220 feet long, propeller-driven, with a 600-ton cargo capacity.

It really was an emblem of the prosperity of the St. Joseph and Benton Harbor area. It was unusual for catering to upper crust passengers and or hauling premium Michigan fruit to Chicago and Milwaukee. Fruit built the Benton Harbor fleet, the mild weather was tailor-made for peaches, grapes, cherries, and pears. Yet the bumper crop was often apples and, because they kept better, they were shipped whenever the lake was navigable. If only her owner had been content to stick with passengers and fruit.

The lure of fat freight fees brought about a deviation from the traditional shipping schedule. The year of 1893 brought bumper crops and a late harvest in the Midwest. This meant that the mills and granaries of Milwaukee were bursting as winter approached. Thousands of tons of flour were still in storage when December storms shut down shipping. Then a mild period in January 1894 encouraged the belief that a few passages to Milwaukee could be safely made.

Well, they made it safely to Milwaukee, but there were many signs that the weather was about to change. All across the Great Lakes there were frantic messages sent for vessels to exercise caution in light of changes suggesting a massive low pressure system. For most vessels on short packet runs or fishing boats offshore of homeport, this meant a few hours at most after a signal or hailing about conditions. Those further away from home had to use discretion and stay moored with cargoes until spring weather allowed them passage home. A few decided to race the storm home. The *Chicora* was one of those.

It came down to a matter of a few hours. Those who had to go from Racine to Chicago, or even Milwaukee to Michigan City, could make such a trip in three to five hours. However, the normal time from Milwaukee to Benton Harbor was more like seven to eight hours. That interval was to be more time than was available. A light springlike rain was falling in the early morning when the

Chicora left Milwaukee. Within three hours, according to those still on the lake at that time, the storm built in intensity to blizzard force with plunging temperatures. Those limping into Chicago southbound from Racine were coated with frozen spray and battered by the twenty to thirty foot ice jams that were driven out into the lake by the high winds.

Those winds built to hurricane force in a few more hours and created a lake surface of watery mountain ranges moving north to south. This was a condition that was extremely hazardous for a heavily loaded vessel on a west to east course. Those on the eastern shore of Lake Michigan that fateful day gave reports of a lone storm-tossed vessel and of distant distress whistles carried on the fierce wind. But such things could only be glimpsed or heard briefly before the low scud of such storms blotted out the view or the scream of the storm filled the ears.

No one knows for certain where the *Chicora* went down or under what type of calamity. No piece of wreckage of the vessel was ever recovered. All hands were lost, not a single body washed up. But shoreline accounts suggest that she almost made it home and was within sight of the St. Joseph River when the pounding waves forced a course change north. Most likely she went down off South Haven. That's where hundreds of barrels of flour were to wash ashore some months later.

In retrospect many found ill omens about the *Chicora's* sailing beyond its unseasonable timing. There was trouble in signing a crew. There was friction between elements of the crew, the product of sometimes violent rivalries between Benton Harbor sailors and St. Joseph sailors. There were fights among the crew before the hawsers were cast off at the beginning of the voyage. There was a certain despondency to the senior crew that was unexplainable. The vessel's captain allegedly got into a big argument at the mill docks in Milwaukee which caused precious hours of delay. But the biggest portent recalled in Benton Harbor was the sad and frightened face of the captain's young son who was making his first lake crossing with his father.

It's a sad, sad story of a tragedy that was quite avoidable if you remove the human lust for profit.

The phantom of the *Chicora* was not immediately seen off the lake. At least no one admitted it for the first few years after she was lost. Supposedly the first one to see her was her owner, the man who arranged her voyage. You can see why he might have been haunted by the disaster. Others subsequently saw her under circumstances that foretold bad luck. Among old fishermen the story developed that a sighting of the phantom *Chicora* was a sign that one's death was imminent.

It hasn't worked that way at all for me. I've seen her once or twice per winter for nearly forty years. Ever since my own father was lost on the lake with my uncle. The irony of their loss of life was that only days before my uncle told me his version of the story of the *Chicora*. He added a twist that I'm sure he invented on the spot. His instant lake lore centered on the allegation that lake men were bodily and soulfully claimed by the *Chicora* because even in the spirit realm she was steaming shorthanded with a green and feuding crew. Don't think that didn't register in my boys' minds when they themselves were claimed by the lake.

So, in more ways than one, I'm seeing family when I see the *Chicora*. I've seen her in my winter walks up toward South Haven and down toward Berrien Springs. I've seen her in icy fog right in the channel of the St. Joseph River. I've heard her sharp whistle on stormy January nights when wind and ice have the lake locked down. I confess I see it in my winter dreams, too.

Of that crew that went down with her in January 1895 I had four ancestors that I know of. Good Benton Harbor men who left families. Families that took generations to recover from the consequences of widowhood and orphanhood that resulted in those cruel times. Generations of hired hands and house girls that followed in the wake of no fathers to steer boys toward a trade or to help young women marry well.

That's why you would never see me out in the lake, not even in an inner tube on a hot January day. The *Chicora* did enough to my kin and kind, she had enough of our spirit and blood on board. When I see her now it's all I can do to not thumb my nose at the old phantom girl. When I was a younger man I was even more vehement about it, shouting, "You won't get me, you deathtrap" and throwing stones toward her. Now I just whisper damnation and return to my warm fireplace. She's done with me and I'm done with her.

Spirit Party on the S.S. Keewatin

S ome lake stories gestate for long periods out of accumulated anecdotes and fragments of research. Others flow from cryptic communications and the search for elusive informants. None are perhaps so sweet as the ones that pop up as surprises when you're not really searching.

Such was the gift given to me in Douglas, Michigan. It was all the more surprising as a ghost story within one of my favorite subgenres, that of the "rowdy ghosts." I first encountered such celebratory groups of spirits in my story collecting efforts in my home turf of Iowa County, Wisconsin. Later efforts would turn up other sturdy examples at LaPointe on Lake Superior's Madeline Island and at many other sites related to the original inhabitants, the French voyageurs, and the pioneers of the early American territories. These origins receive homage at the rendezvous reenactment camps of modern day "buckskinners," and it is at such encampments that I heard many representative stories of this type.

Rowdy ghosts are an exuberant lot. As with the first group I encountered at Old Helena on the banks of the Wisconsin River, they exist in a more or less recurrent loop of card playing, hard drinking, womanizing, and fighting. Usually they manifest as noisy arguments at outdoor sites of old abandoned settlements. Occasionally they still roam as gangs in the wee hours on streets of sleepy villages. Rarely, but dramatically, they are seen as dueling partisans ripe with the wounds of a century or two of musket balls and saber slashes.

Ann saw something quite different from that. I am grateful that she was not too busy scooping ice cream when I ordered a cone in Douglas, Michigan. I am also grateful that her rosy Dutch face broke into a pretty smile after my answer to her small talk about what might bring me around Lake Michigan.

*   *   *

Oh, have I got a ghost story for you. I don't think you could see them right now, but you could visit the place where I've seen them. Just go to Tower Marine, off the Blue Star Highway, along the Kalamazoo River. There you'll find the *S.S. Keewatin*. It's a museum now and for the price of admission you can tour all decks, some of the cabins and staterooms, and the bridge. Dad took me there a few years ago.

It's very large for a lake passenger ship, longer than a football field I would guess. It still looks very pretty inside and out. The interior is especially polished and gleaming. The very first time on board I could almost see the wealthy passengers walking the decks and the crisply uniformed stewards attending to passenger whims. It's not hard to imagine that scene at all. Or to hear the tinkling sound of crystal wine goblets and fine china in the dining room.

Of course I've never experienced such things, I've hardly ever left Douglas. But even here we can watch old movies about the wealthy on cruises. I hoped for some of that flavor on tour boats on my few visits to Chicago and Detroit. But it usually feels more like a bus on water. Maybe someday I'll take a winter trip to the Caribbean and take a real cruise.

I sure could use a break from ice cream scooping, burger flipping, and cottage cleaning. That's been the only work for me in Douglas and its pretty much what we've always done in our family, work the tourist business and take care of the summer residents. That's been going on in Douglas for over a hundred years. Dad said his grandfathers were fishermen, but the fishing slacked off years ago. I've been staying around to take care of Dad, he's a disabled World War II veteran and I was the youngest, the "late baby," of the family.

But I like it here. I don't think I could live in the cities like my sisters do. Or work in the factories like my brothers do. I like the quiet. I like to take walks alone. You can do that here in Douglas, even as a woman at night. That's how I first saw the ghosts on the *S.S. Keewatin*.

It was an unseasonably hot summer night. We don't get many of those, or at least we didn't until recent years. Maybe three or four nights of still air in a summer. Usually we have the breezes. I've never had an air conditioner in my trailer. Anyway, it was hot, very hot, and I couldn't sleep. Walking was always my solution to that problem.

I can walk four to five miles an hour. Though that night it was so hot I kind of shuffled along in my sandals. I thought maybe it would be cooler by the water so I walked down to Tower Marine. It was late and the business office was closed. At a distance I thought I heard voices, but I thought it was just some late night beer drinking on some of the private boats docked there. When I got closer I saw that the lights of a *S.S. Keewatin* were on. It could have been some late night maintenance. Instead, it was a party.

The first thought in my mind was that it had been rented out for a private affair. Maybe for a wedding reception or even for a bachelor party. As I got closer though, I could see that everyone was dressed like they were from the 1920s. Still, it could have been a costume party.

Then I heard the oldtime music from an orchestra and saw the men and women dancing. What finally told me what I was dealing with was when the music stopped, the ship's lights blinked off, and the crowd chatter stopped. There was no one there!

At first I didn't tell anyone about it, especially Dad. He's on a short fuse about UFOs and conspiracy theories, so I thought he'd take a dim view of any talk about dancing ghosts. I thought, at best, he might suggest I needed a date and set me up with one of the younger guys at his veterans post. Been there, done that. A date with those middle aged boonie humpers is just an exercise in designated driving. At worst, I thought he might think me crazy. He already thinks two-thirds of the population should be institutionalized or medicated. I guess I wondered myself if I was seeing things. But I thought not, I'm pretty grounded.

Later that summer, on another walk, I heard that orchestra sound coming from the ship again. But it stopped before I got over that way. It stopped abruptly in mid-note like the night I was down there. The second experience gave me a little more confidence that something supernatural was going on.

Eventually I got up the courage to tell a girlfriend. Kim told me she overheard a conversation where one of the summer residents was talking about a similar thing. So, she said, she had to see for herself and went down there about three in the morning. Nothing! So she went down again, not once, not twice, but five more times before she ran into anything. Kim's a stubborn girl. On that sixth trip she thought she saw the ship lit up and with well-dressed people at the railing. But as soon as she got closer the ship went dark and silent. Still, it made a believer out of her.

At least now I had somebody who believed me. Together we

tried to sneak up on the ship again for the next two summers without any luck. The third summer we ran into an old hermit lady who lives out in the woods. When I was a girl we were told she was a witch. But darn if she didn't know the whole story.

The old lady told us things about the *S.S. Keewatin* we never knew. That it was built in Scotland. That it first was an excursion boat for a Canadian railroad. And she ticked off the names of famous passengers from its glory days. But the names meant nothing to me. I mean secretary so-and-so in President Taft's cabinet or the head of the DeSoto automobile company. All the while I'm thinking who's Taft and what's a De Soto.

But she set us straight on the who and what of the ship. She said she had seen the same spirits out in the dunes where the old sawmill town of Singapore used to be. It turned into a ghost town a hundred years ago. The old lady said those ghosts often celebrate out at that old site. Her theory is that these ghosts of loggers, millworkers, maids, and tavern girls somehow get to put on good clothes and party on the *S.S. Keewatin*.

After I mulled over awhile I worked up the courage to ask Dad about Singapore. Eventually I told him the whole story. I was surprised when he didn't explode. Instead he nodded and told me about ghosts of lost buddies he saw after the Battle of the Bulge in Europe. He said he's seen them almost every winter since. He just nodded and said anything's possible.

One of these times I'm going to sneak up on that old ship. Maybe even creep up there and join the dance. Whatya doing tonight?

Man with the Branded Hand

Crossover in legends and lore between waters salt and fresh was once common on the Great Lakes. Considerable numbers of New England seafarers and fishermen made their way to the large inland seas after the opening of the Northwest Territories. Immigrants from Europe's northern coasts and isles then arrived after the territories became states. The maritime stories of all these peoples mingled with those of the tribal first inhabitants to create new narratives on the inland waters.

Later, the peoples connected to the Big Sisters of Superior, Huron, and Michigan were to contribute their sons to the merchant and naval fleets of Canada and the United States in no small numbers. Many of these seafarers from lake country became well-known in the waterfront haunts of the world as reliable and stalwart sailors. Many a rough first mate and crusty petty officer of the sea had his roots by the large inland waters and offered solicitude to young sailors of similar origin. Some of these men became legend and left their marks from the frigid arctic to the balmy tropics. When these men returned home from the long voyages and visits to exotic ports they brought more maritime lore home with them. Thus the Great Lakes narrative was ever kept fresh and linked to brethren of the water everywhere.

One of the favorite types of seafarer stories told in fishnet shanties, boathouses, and harbor taverns was that of the resolute and manly captain. There were, to be sure, also stories of scoundrel captains and rigid disciplinarians of the sea. But the captains who lived on in the hearts of sailors, freshwater and saltwater, were those whose seamanship and courage was impressed by example, not by force.

Some such legendary men retired from the sea to lake country. Most had kin who plied the inland waters. Some were non-natives who received grants of land in lake country from satisfied shipping companies. Others ended up in our midst by circumstances unknown or accidental.

Peter, a Muskegon, Michigan, teacher, who restores old boats, knows about one such sea hero who came to lake country. He knows the circumstances and reasons for the sea captain's settlement near Lake Michigan. He also knows the legacy of pain that surrounds this hero's life — and afterlife.

*   *   *

Firm and fair, that's what maritime men thought of Captain Walker. That's Jonathan Walker who came to this area after the Civil War. In those days he was quite famous. You might say that he was a hero to many other famous people. He was an exemplar of the finest ideals and morals in a republic of free men.

Captain Walker had an excellent reputation as a seaman and ship's master long before he became known to the public. He was one of those captains who attracted a crew where other captains created fear and loathing. Old salts felt comfortable signing their young sons onto his crews, reckoning that Captain Walker's disposition and skill would heighten the chance that a young man would return home safely. Though not lenient concerning infractions, he abhorred physical punishment, favoring instead confinement and double duty. He was a prudent man, content to persuade shipowners that a delayed cargo was preferable to a lost cargo, who believed loss of crew a breach of sacred trust.

So it was that sailors knew of Captain Walker before the public at large knew him. It was likely that he might never have gained any notoriety among those who insist upon firm footing had he not taken up the burning issue of the mid-1800s. I refer to slavery and its abolition.

Understand that sea captains tended toward the amoral where commercial interests were involved. There had been a long tradition of slave hauling, almost three centuries on the high seas. Even longer if you go back to the coastal waters of ancient times. Sea captains travel far and wide and tend to see many things done differently than their own upbringing instructs them. A man in this position seldom goes far if he rebels against the prevailing culture and mode of commerce. Shipowners are also generally intolerant of views that do not serve their bottom line.

Still, by the 1840s the tide was clearly running against slavery. This issue was taken up in many port city pulpits. Educated captains, of which there were more than a few, read the tracts and books commonly available. Captain Walker was one such man taken up by the passion for justice that motivated the abolitionist fervor.

At first, he was not outspoken; instead he showed a dockside preference for free labor in the ports of the American South and made
efforts to find cargoes without the taint of slavery.

It was said he became more active by stages. His supporters said
this was true to his pattern of cautious exploration of possibilities.
His detractors, without proof, made the wild allegation that his
growing boldness related to the financial inducement of abolition-
ists. The stories suggest that he was in the early 1840s smuggling
the occasional slave out of the American South to free Caribbean
territory. The same stories indicate that by the mid-1840s he was
providing passage to whole extended families of slaves, sometimes
even larger groups.

This is a largely unknown segment of the paths to freedom from
slavery. Nearly everyone's heard of the Underground Railroad, the
network of anti-slavery Americans who spirited runaway slaves to
safety. But there is no mention of a counterpart "underwater ferry,"
a network of seafarers and port residents who made arrangements
for runaways to hide in cargo holds. Yet such activity did occur.

Captain Walker stepped into the eye of this political storm when
he boldly took a group of slaves from Florida to British territory in
the Bahamas. Captains were sometimes simply slapped on the wrist
when they professed no knowledge of their human cargo. But Captain Walker did not disavow his actions. For this he was arrested
upon returned to the U.S. for multiple violations of the Fugitive
Slave Act. He was quickly tried, convicted, fined, pilloried, impris-
oned, and, true to the grotesque code of the South, branded with a
hot iron with the letters "S.S." on his right hand. This proclaimed
him a slave stealer, not a human liberator.

This cruel act outraged northerners and many Europeans. Upon
his release he became a celebrity and a public speaker much in demand. He remained a humble man, minimizing his suffering and
eloquently pointing out that his ordeal was nothing, compared to
the horrors of slavery. Almost everyone of the day who identified
with the abolitionist cause knew his name. He was viewed as a
living martyr to the cause of the budding Free Soil and Republican
movements. Poet John Greenleaf Whittier wrote the moving "Man
with the Branded Hand" about Captain Walker.

So how did this eminent and honorable man come to reside in
the Muskegon area? This question still generates discussion. Some
suggest a connection to an abolitionist benefactor. Some suggest
another financial tie or arrangement. I've even heard a claim about

an inheritance from a remote relative. Perhaps there's a grain of truth in one or more of these versions. But in our family the explanation went back to the sea.

I had a great uncle who claimed that we had an ancestor who shipped with Captain Walker back in those troubled times. Apparently our ancestor was one of those Lake Michigan boys who regale entire shipboard companies with tales about the beauties of the fair lands, along the lakes, the gentle springs, the sweet summers, and the rich autumns ripe with fruits of tree and vine. One of that kind who awhile aboard his vessel has the idyllic vision of his homelands continually in his mind's eye and who nevertheless yearns for the sea by his second day at home.

My great uncle said it was this sailor's praises on behalf of western Michigan that brought Captain Walker to an orchard at Lake Harbor. Here Walker found congenial maritime company, land prices within his means, and enterprise fit for a country gentleman. My ancestor did indeed succeed in convincing the good captain that Lake Harbor was a suitable place to spend one's post-sailing retirement years. Walker soon became a valued member of the community even though he was no longer a national figure.

Captain Walker sought no attention, but it continued to seek him. He was much in demand as a speaker by the Grange, business groups, church organizations, and lakefarers' associations. It was also known that he persisted in his concern over the costs of human bondage even after the formal freeing of the slaves. It was said that he continued to help in the reuniting of families who had been dispersed by the Underground Railroad, particularly those whose runaway members had crossed the lakes to Canada.

At this point, so said my great uncle, we have a blending of history and legend. Captain Walker died in 1877 with modest means. The community mourned him as no other, particularly the sizable sectors of Scandinavian communities involved in the lake trades who knew of his heroism. Word of his death became known in national circles and none less than William LLoyd Garrison determined that Muskegon had insufficiently memorialized Walker and commenced a national subscription drive to build a monument to the captain. In due course the monument was placed in Evergreen Cemetery on Pine Street in Muskegon. The stone has the hand with the "S.S." carved on it.

Almost immediately after Captain Walker's death there were stories about abnormal happenings at the gravesite. An innocent young boy reported that an old man in sea captain's garb appeared in the dusk and asked to be shown the way toward the lake. Others reported that the aroma of salty sea air was something noticeable at the Monument. In more than one account, groups of freedmen were alleged to have made pilgrimages to the site, only to never reemerge from the cemetery. One terrified cemetery sexton claimed that a hand with a "S.S." brand appeared up out of the ground after news of the political deals that unraveled Reconstruction in the South and opened the door to racist terror.

I asked my great uncle if he had seen or experienced any of those things. He hemmed and he hawed, allowing as he'd always been on the fringe of such happenings. But he knew personally and believed those whose senses did perceive such things. For his part, he had only one brush with odd sensations out at Evergreen Cemetery. While there on Memorial Day, a major social obligation in those days, he revisited the monument and smelled the unmistakable odor of burning flesh. The smell one might smell at the branding of human skin. Thereafter, he had lifelong dreams about the branded hand upon a ship's wheel.

I've only had one such dream come to me and it happened 10,000 miles away. I was a gunner's mate on a patrol boat in Vietnam's brownwater fleet. I had many times when I was scared and many times when I had to worry about doing the right thing. At one particularly troubling juncture I had a dream of a chart of Lake Michigan. In the dream a hand came into view and placed an old compass on the chart right at Muskegon's location. When the hand moved I saw the "S.S." quite clearly. When I woke up I knew that if I followed the values that I grew up with I would make it back here.

Echoes of the Car Ferries

Mention of the term "car ferry" triggers the assumption among many unfamiliar with Great Lakes history that the reference is to ships bearing automobiles. Though they served the region until recent times, there is no generalized memory of the large freighter ferries that were once an integral part of the transportation network. Even the rail fans who remember the latter stages of operations for the Chicago and Northwestern Railroad at Manitowoc, Wisconsin, know little about the glory years of such traffic when the ferries steamed regularly from an assortment of homeports. Those without familiarity with rail systems often express wonder that such sailings offered economies, both financial and timewise.

While the number of vessels so engaged was never anywhere near the level of the iron or grain trade, the freightcar ferries left an indelible stamp of lakefaring culture. This was especially true on Lake Michigan where even at an early date there were many translake ties and an incentive to avoid the bottleneck of Chicago. The ferry operators had to design their own equipment, which was large by lake standards. They also took pains to hire experienced masters and crews as it was expected that the ferries would operate beyond the normal shipping season.

Only lakefarers now remember the challenges of the ferry navigation. Among the dwindling numbers of former ferry crewmen are those with sharp memories and appreciation for the history of their maritime niche. Roscoe is one such ferry veteran who remains eager to tell the tales. On the day I met him on the dock of Ludington, Michigan, the look in his eye when the approaching ferry gave a blast of the air horn told me that his heart was still out on the lake.

*   *   *

Ferries operated on blood, guts, and cold steel. No one remembers that. No one remembers the toll paid in life and limb. These ferry operations combined two very dangerous trades: maritime and rail. Add to that the unseasonable operations on this cold-hearted lake and you have a formula for danger with a capital "D."

No one understood this better than the ferrymen of Ludington. We had it in our blood. Three, four generations of ferrymen in some families and plenty of relatives working auxiliary trades on the docks and on the car-switching crews. It was a key role in Midwest trade and development. It held together the otherwise separated parts of the Great Lakes.

In a way it all got its start before railroads reached the lakeports. There was a time when package freighters carried crates, and barrels, and bulk goods that were transported by wagon to the docks on one side of the lakes and put back on wagons on the other side. This was done with food, hardware, lumber, lead bars, and pig iron.

Then when the railroads became the main ground transport, the old break load and reload methods were used as before. Naturally by then the loads were much bigger and more involved. This meant a tremendous amount of labor was required at all stages. This put shipping at the mercy of labor shortages, labor disruptions, and other human factors. This is why the thinkers and engineers had to devise a way to get the railcars themselves across the lake without handling the loads on the docks.

The leaders in these developments were at Grand Trunk Railway. Now there's a name hardly anybody remembers today. They built some of the first heavy-duty freightcar ferry facilities, figured out the design and operation of landing facilities, and caused to be built some of the sturdy prototype vessels. There were all sorts of engineering problems to be solved. How do you keep a level track line into a ship that is rising or falling due to loads or waves? How do you keep railroad cars from careening about in heavy seas? How do you manage motive power so as to not put the locomotive's weight on the edge of the dock or on the ferry itself?

It was Grand Trunk that first learned many of the hard lessons that others benefitted from and later incorporated into general ferry operations. They learned that you could push a ferry away from a dock and dump rolling stock into the drink. They learned that a flexible tracked apron was needed to connect dock and ferry lest you derail cars right on the vessel. They learned the bitter lessons, as with the loss of the *Milwaukee* with all hands, of properly securing cars and bolstering seagates. These were the lessons of the 1890s and early 1900s when freightcar ferries were just coming into their own.

It was in Ludington that this industrial knowledge was taught and preserved. We were situated such as to be a hub of ferry operations. But it was more than a matter of location. It was more a matter of temperament, perhaps even genetics. Ferries were our life and only the good people of Manitowoc, Wisconsin, had even a hint of how life can revolve about such things.

In our town so much of it revolved around the Pere Marquette Line. They were the industry standard. The first of the real freightcar ferries in that line was the *Pere Marquette #15*, a sturdy steel vessel. The fleet of freightcar ferries would eventually grow to twelve vessels, which meant they were often meeting each other on passages and even helping each other when in distress. As far as I know, there was nothing else like this in North America.

In terms of legend and lore, these vessels left big wakes in the magical waters of Lake Michigan. The *Pere Marquette #15* itself, or should I say its specter, has been seen on moonless nights, standing about two miles offshore from here. The ferry line lost men in many circumstances and their souls wandered back to Ludington, too. Even dockside there were deck hands crushed in the apron and brakemen dismembered in the car movements. I've met people who know nothing at all about the ferries or the freight cars who have seen the specters of the men and the equipment.

I had one man, a tourist, recently describe railroad equipment he claimed to have seen here the night before. What he saw were "helper flats," the old-fashioned wood deck flatcars that were used to push loaded freight cars onto the ferry so the engine did not cross the apron. I told him that those things had not seen use in years. He asked how that could be and when I told him how people have seen the ghostly images of things past connected to the freightcar ferries, he just looked at me kind of funny.

I have no idea how that sort of thing would work. Does a long gone ferry have a spirit? Does a piece of scrapped railroad equipment have a certain vibration which gives it a second lease on life on the visual spectrum? I don't know how one finds answers when the subject falls into that gap between science and superstition. Now I believe in a spirit existence outside what we call normal life. I just don't know how one accounts for such things. It could be a type of energy that comes out of the essence of things or maybe out of the "charge" we give them through our focus on them at certain points in time.

I've heard some say that it's the lake itself. I've heard others say it's the Ludington-Manitowoc connection. Lake Michigan is a powerful physical feature on the Earth. Think of the energy it soaks up from the sun and other places. Think about the power generated by wave action. Maybe there's an energy connection, an electromagnetic grid that accounts for odd things that flow from Manitowoc to Ludington.

We had one little tricky thing like this that was at work when we were working the Northwestern to Chesapeake and Ohio connection. That was the last of the mixed freightcar, automobile, and passenger loads. That was the thirty freightcar and one-hundred and fifty auto configuration. We had a time when we would keep seeing a '57 Chevy get on in Manitowoc. It was a beauty. The men would want to check it out. But it seems we were always missing it on the Ludington offload. I thought we simply got busy and overlooked it. But one time it was positioned such that it should have been last off. I watched closely. It never made it to Ludington.

That was the only thing I ever experienced personally on the old freightcar ferries. But other men, ferrymen and railroaders, told me about other weird stuff. Lifeboats and wheelhouses of long ago wrecked vessels that would appear on the car deck and quickly disappear. After the freightcar ferries stopped running you didn't hear much about such things. The remaining ferry only hauled vehicles and passengers.

I made one round trip on that ferry. On the way back from Manitowoc I went down one passageway that wasn't meant for passengers. I passed a rough looking group in the shadows and thought it odd that they weren't occupied with the details of a ferry soon to offload. An old scruffy fellow among them had a canvas bag marked with the faint stencil of the *Milwaukee.* I thought to myself, you can't keep a good ferryman off the lakes even after he's gone down.

Legends of the Sleeping Bear

It is almost impossible to separate the stories of the Great Lakes from the oral traditions of the first inhabitants. The American Indian narrative is, of course, much older than the first impressions recorded in the journals of French missionaries and British traders. Some of these ancient tales have roots going back to the last Ice Age and the formation of the lakes. Others evolved over centuries out of complex intertribal relations and lengthy migrations.

Many of the oldest Great Lakes stories arise out of aboriginal cosmologies that are little understood or appreciated among European Americans. This spiritual context establishes a linkage between the subject matter, the location, and an overarching sense of sacred place. The stories often serve as a native version of Genesis and Exodus. And like Christian/Judaic/Islamic holy writ of Middle Eastern origins, the traditions can serve as creation stories, general moral instructions, and political frameworks. Many of these stories are very layered in their original meanings.

Of all the early Great Lakes peoples the group often called the Chippewa had the most geographically dispersed stories. They were among the most recent of the pre-European westward migrations, and their journey as a people put them on intimate terms with almost every inch of the Great Lakes basin, from the mouth of the St. Lawrence to the portages to the rivers of North America's interior. The battles of the fur wars took their canoes back eastward along their ancient route. In this way stories about special places received continued vitality.

Maxwell is not the only one in the Glen Arbor area whose roots go back to the early times on the lakes. But he is one of the few prepared to acknowledge the tie of blood and spirit.

*   *   *

Sleeping Bear Dune has a story tradition that is at least a thousand years old among the Anishinabe, the Chippewa peoples who are better identified as Ojibwe, Ottawa, and Potawatomi. We have families here of all those native nations who intermarried and as-similated at an early stage. But not all of us forgot the old traditions.

I'll often use the word "legends" to describe those traditional stories. But when the old medicine men come down from Canada to visit they call the same traditions "sacred teachings." It's amazing how similar the traditions of the various parts of the Anishinabe are, even though the contact between groups has been limited for many years. Those medicine men are amazing, too, they can find a household that is part Indian or a powerful spiritual place without ever having been in lower Michigan before.

The basic tradition is about how the Sleeping Bear Dunes and the nearby islands formed. When this earth was young, when North America was still Turtle Island, things were just coming into being. Even the geologists will tell you that Sleeping Bear Dune is very unusual, probably the largest evolving dune in North America. When the Anishinabe first saw it on the westward migration they were very impressed. People close to the earth know instinctively that such a formation is the result of strong primal forces. So it was natural to conclude that it possesses a spirit of its own.

Anishinabe elders explained Sleeping Bear Dune as a mother bear who swam across Lake Michigan with her cubs, but reached shore without the little ones. She mourned them, kept waiting for them by the lake, and eventually turned into a dune. Out of pity and recognizing her loyalty, the Gitchi Manitou, the Great Spirit, raised the cubs in the form of North Manitou Island and South Manitou Island.

That's a simple enough story, isn't it? Let's take it piece by piece. Here we have a questing people, people on a long journey. Among them are impatient explorers, brave men willing to risk hardship. What happens if the young, the old, and the weak are hurried along on this journey? They are lost like the cubs.

Here you have people following the directions of prophecy, but who nevertheless have curiosity that pulls them in all directions. Some say that the other Algonquin peoples of the Midwest were offshoots of this journey and that they peeled off from the main group. Might not an ill-omen in story form keep some to the main shoreline path and discourage groups from trans-lake crossings?

So, yes, this is a cautionary tale. But it is also a tale of waiting, patience, and devotion to purpose. It is a tale that deals with con-flicting needs and impulses. Take care with the children on the journey, we journey for them! Know the journey will entail sacrifice, but do not allow loss and grieving on the way to turn you into a dune that cannot move on its own! Be careful, but keep going!

Some of the old medicine men say that Sleeping Bear Dune and the two islands were signposts in the migration journey, signals to turn northward and westward. But they also say the islands had a place in spiritual evolution of the Anishinabe. South Manitou Island and North Manitou Island were not places of year round habitation. But they were places where a young person might go for a vision, to talk to the elders of the past, and to listen to the lessons of the Great Spirit. Out there they found different medicine for men and women, different lessons for those called to the spirit path and those called to the warrior path.

I guess all these feelings among the people about the power of this place contributed to everything that has happened in this area ever since. That takes in everything from Point Betsie Lighthouse to Good Harbor Bay. Between those points and the islands you have a hundred square miles of powerful spirit medicine where you can see things that are hard to see otherwise. The Europeans call such places haunted, but people close to the spirits of the land call such places sacred places. It's true that some old legends talk about evil spirits in a place, but the wise old ones will tell you that all things that you are allowed to experience are gifts from the Great Spirit. Even if the gift comes in the form of a challenge or test.

That's why European Americans see different things around here than an old Anishinabe might. And if not actually different things, then different interpretations of the same things. Lighthouse keepers at Point Betsie saw a face in the big waves that came in with the storms. The same face is seen in the large waves of all the Great Lakes, especially up on Huron and Superior. It is the Great Spirit manifesting itself in the power of the lake. A man separated from the earth might see this as a threatening demon. But a man who seeks to learn from the lake might be humbled by the privilege of the power revealing itself.

Someone ill at ease with the sounds of nature might find moaning and screeching out on the two islands. Someone open to nature's teachings might find a beautiful lyric language and deep meaning in the same sounds. A very few, those most attuned to the communication of spirits, will even find the silences between the sounds and understand how they connect the sounds.

The legend of South Manitou Island is one of dangerous beauty.

It once had a cathedral of towering trees. I have heard that bold young women once used it for their rites and ceremonies. Some brokenhearted among them returned there to find final refuge. These spirits can make the island a tricky place. Now I won't go as far as to claim that those maidens are like the German Lorelei, but South Manitou Island has been a magnet for shipwrecks. Some like the *Francisco Morizon* were brought aground by storms. But perhaps more were pulled too close by curiosity or some other lure. Add to that some strange behaviors and desires among those who kept the lighthouse at the south end and you have a case for the siren's call.

North Manitou Island has different properties. It has the character of the North, the place of contemplation. This is where powerful medicine men came at the end of their earthly existence. It was always a place where the great change of life back to the dust of the earth was close at hand and whispered like a friend to those who knew its language. The European Americans called the great change "death" and they shivered on North Manitou Island as they cut the trees and listened to death's voice in the wind. So even now, say the old Anishinabe, that island should only be visited by strong spiritual warriors who are prepared to know the great change. They will come back even stronger if they survive.

But the most powerful spirit medicine in the area is the Sleeping Mother herself. Her spirit is still strong and her healing can touch those who are troubled at heart. So I was told by the elders. They said the spirit there can help anyone who feels abandoned, especially young ones who lost a mother. That's why an elder had me sleep out on the dune long ago.

It is like he told me, the spirits could haunt you if you let them. He also said that if you let the sacredness of this place enter your heart then the spirits will help you, not haunt you.

Fishtown's Shivaree

Traditions and odd rituals pop up in the hauntings all across rural America. There is something about the vanishing ways of our forebears that seems to resonate within tales of the supernatural. One is never quite sure if the wistfulness and nostalgia is within the heart of the observer or within the spirit manifestation itself. It is safe to assume that in many cases the longing, regret, and sense of loss reside in both places.

Fewer and fewer young Americans know anything about the rich life of local quirky celebrations, often rooted in ethnic identity, that blessed every corner of the continent not long ago. Very few feel such folkways in their bones and experience the seasonal pull of them as tidal forces within their bodies. Fewer still know the obscure wisdom and hidden meanings within the archaic customs, whisperings from ancestors at least medieval and, perhaps, neolithic.

Thus the posture of young Eric is unusual in its fervor and its understanding. His peers know of times past chiefly from books and historical reenactments, but his family has steeped him in the mood and chronology of the Leland area to the point where it seems to be implanted in him at the cellular level. One almost gets the impression that he may have a presence within him that has come back from those long gone days. Enthused or possessed? Decide for yourself.

* * *

Every day I find out more about how things were. It's just interesting how it all fits together. Sometimes I can just visualize it. It's like I'm rediscovering it inside myself, like it's been there the whole time waiting to wake up.

Maybe it comes from my mom's side, Especially her father. They laugh and call that the "French side," with a whole bunch of kidding about Cajuns, Canucks, sardine-eaters, and squaw-bundlers. They didn't mind joking about their roots, but would raise a fuss if an outsider did the same. Grandfather would proudly say that our ancestors had been thrown out of every province in Canada and most of the Great Lakes states.

He claimed that we're descendants of Antoine Manseau, the big-wig who founded the original village and built a lumber empire. Manseau left sons who brought other businesses to Leland. They brought in French Canadian fishermen and craftsmen. Families like Martineau, Batteau, and DuBois. In our line we had every-thing from educated men of culture to mixed blood illegitimate sons of old voyaguers. The family trades followed the economic ebb and flow of Leland's economic development. Anything from loggers and ironworkers to gamblers and grifters.

Grandfather taught me quite a bit about the old times and the old ways, but he left me an appetite for more. So I've read every-thing I can get my hands on and I've talked to almost every elderly person around Leland. My interest in the subject drives me, but there's part of me that misses the old man and hears a little of his voice in these other old-timers. Plus they fill in the gaps about things my grandfather didn't know much about, like some of the old build-ings.

Grandfather was focused mostly on traditions and more particu-larly about Fishtown traditions, Fishtown is unique. When you look at it you might only see wind-beaten and graying fishing shacks at the mouth of the Carp River. But it's really a look into the past, a remnant of the look and feel of every fishing village from Presque Isle on Erie to Bayfield on Superior. As far as I know, it's the only intact original collection of 1800s dock buildings, net houses, ice shacks, and repair sheds. It's the 1890s when you walk among them. I can feel, hear, and smell it.

But Grandfather knew it was much more than that, more than just buildings. It's where his ancestors worked and played, where they met, mingled and intermarried until we were a stew of French, Norwegian, and every other lake bloodline. He knew of the bless-ings of the catch that were given by pastors. He could tell you about how a fishing boat crew needed the season's new wine for luck. He could tell you old stories that had been handed down from Normandy, Nova Scotia, Scandinavian fjord country, and North Sea islands.

Of all those things he talked about, the one that pleased him most to talk about was the Frenchman's Shivaree. Kind of a bach-elor party among fishermen that would start the night before a wedding and continue until daylight the morning after the wed-ding. This made it roughly a thirty-six hour celebration. He felt it embodied the French Canadian lake spirit. He said it was the only thing left of the old ways that the spirits of Fishtown could get through to us. He claimed that late at night he could still hear the racket of a shivaree, still hear the drinking songs and fiddle of the party on the dock. He took me down to Fishtown shortly before he died and I heard something, too. It was faint, but I definitely heard it.

That's what later made me anxious to dig into this tradition. I found out that the shivaree is not quite the French tradition that Grandfather described. It has some European roots in the romantic concept of chivalry, but was Americanized in so many ways. I found loads of stories about it that go all the way back to American colonial times. Back then the biggest practitioners of the shivaree were Scotch-Irish and Pennsylvania Dutch. Not much in the way of French influence unless you count the Alsatian French Huguenots who were absorbed by the Pennsylvania Dutch. These groups passed it on to others and it spread west with the pioneers, popping up in Montana and New Mexico during cattle drive days.

Knowing that Grandfather did not know the whole story or tradition did not spoil it for me. It just made me eager to find out more about the customs and what they meant. It made me more able to hear those old shivarees down in Fishtown and figure out how they worked. As I learn more I think I hear those old shivaree ghosts more clearly.

They have a pattern you know. The custom was to start in Fishtown after dark. That's where they started drinking with the groom, getting him drunk. Then they would hoist the groom on their shoulders and parade him down to the Harbor House around midnight and play a jug and washtub band until they were driven off by people throwing rotten things and chamber pots at them. They would then continue the parade around the town and demand more drinks at the houses of the groom's uncles. A smart uncle would simply leave the booze on the porch. This went on until sunup when they would deposit the groom, usually a lot worse for the wear, back on his doorstep. The shivaree party would retreat to Fishtown, drink up until the wedding, and then parade back to the church. After relative silence during the wedding service, they would crank up the jug band after the bride and groom came out the door.

It didn't stop there. They acted as escort for the bride and groom on their way to the wedding dance and dinner. There they made great fools of themselves and often some of them had to be locked up in stable grain bins until morning. At the end of the dance the shivaree group escorted the bride and groom to their quarters and provided a late night serenade until they were again driven off by thrown garbage. The remaining hardy souls then went back to Fishtown to finish their night of celebration. It was certainly a young man's sport.

It seems that the real life custom waned as other more temperance-minded groups moved into Leland and as fishing declined. But it's still there in the spirits of Fishtown for anybody so inclined to tap into it. I've heard it. And one of these nights I'm going to take a bottle down there and join in.

Old Mission Mysteries

O ld Mission Peninsula is an easy place to miss on a Lake Michigan circumnavigation. It's an odd land form that is set back within Grand Traverse Bay. It's out of view of deep water lakefarers. It's also easy enough to miss by ground transportation unless you spot Highway 37 running north out of Traverse City.

The peninsula also offers something different in terms of supernatural fare. Instead of one type of occurrence, it boosts a whole complex of odd happenings and inexplicable phenomena. This includes the usual haunted houses and landmarks with spirit presences. But also among the reports one finds a potpourri of the paranormal. In my brief time in these environs I heard accounts about strange creatures, UFOs, secret government activity, and grave robbing.

Collectors of strange stories are always at a disadvantage when gauging the veracity and sincerity of sources of brief acquaintance. This is especially true when their accounts are at odds and filled with the lilt of competitive and proprietary attitudes. So it was that I settled on Bradford's account. He not only seemed the respectable sweater-clad gentleman on a shoreline walk at the point of the peninsula, he was the only talkative source who did not elevate one set of tales over another. In such things an open mind is a welcome refuge.

* * *

The reason you hear so many different accounts is because of the nature of the place. It's a different physical space. Some would say it has different physical properties. Supposedly the old Ottawa people knew of a presence within this peninsula, supposedly the peninsula itself was some sort of pointer. But to what or where has been lost over time.

Some of this may have something to do with those more recent notions of place. You know, the ideas of sacred place, of power places, and electro-magnetic fields. This is all new stuff for me, yet I felt I had to read up on it just to make sense of these different stories I was hearing. It doesn't pay to judge the theories behind these different explanations. The truth may be a very complex thing.

What holds us back more is the marginal nature of many of the people who come forward with these reports. The fellow who sees UFOs off the point is in the bag half the time and is known to be overly fond of bourbon. Then we have one redneck bunch who claims to see a bigfoot sort of thing, but they're our local suspected poachers and dognappers. We even have a lady who says the peninsula is a base for angels, at least when she's not under her doctor's care and medicated.

So we have an uphill battle on some of this. Yet you need to sort out the stories from the sources. Sure you need to take their conditions and temperaments into account. Their faults don't preclude some kernel of truth in those tales. Even a blind squirrel finds a nut on occasion.

Let's get down to some of these things that are going on out here. We can start with the stuff right out here on the point. The first would be involving the Old Mission Lighthouse. The structure has odd stories associated with it all the way back to its construction in 1870. Even when it was being built the construction laborers had experiences of strange presences. I've heard those experiences talked about as "the cold hand." In other words, the builders and the lighthouse keepers felt the sensation of an icy cold touch. Then were the lights too. Now you'll say we're all goofy — lights in a lighthouse, like coal in New Castle. Well, it was a different light, not the beacon, more of a glow. Sometimes it seemed like it emanated from the entire structure. I saw it myself many years ago.

Then there are the creature stories. Most of them of the big foot variety, but other stuff too. Some like sea-monsters and others like mythical beasts. And not all of the sources here are unreliable. You get the feeling they've seen something out of the ordinary. Who knows, exotic animal escapees from game farms or laboratories? Or odd pets that have outgrown their owners' capabilities. For some reason most of those sightings occur on the cove on the west side of the peninsula.

The UFO stuff is a little murkier. I don't hear as much about it anymore. It was more common a decade or two ago. Some said it had something to do with the Air Force base up north. That may have had something to do with the patterns here. It was always a low level buzzing, always on a north-south axis. Some said that these fly-bys were associated with a glow farther out in the lake proper.

We also have the Old Mission House. This is a structure of early origin, maybe 1840. As the name implies, it was part of the plying of the religion trade. In this case Presbyterians of a dour bent intent on saving American Indian souls. Their Ottawa and Chippewa charges were far too casual about such matters and some friction resulted in the cultural clash. One must remember that missions of that day we're not always content to let God's love act as instructional incentive. There was, even among clergy, a tendency toward coercion, maybe even the lash. There is rumor that a physically abused young Indian expired on those premises and continues to haunt it.

The Old Mission Church had its hauntings too. At least the original one did. It was the Presbyterian church building erected in 1839. It was for the conversion of the Chippewa and Ottawa who were left in the area. There again is the issue of whether disease and hunger impressed them into obedience to a vengeful God. In any event, there was sometimes heard a choir of American Indian children singing hymns in their native tongue. Old-timers reported this to me with some frequency about the original church. What's there now is a replica and I've never heard about the voices in there, but a few people claim to have heard the choir in the general vicinity in more recent times.

Back to the Old Mission Lighthouse. There you have a slew of different things supposedly going on besides that glow that I saw and the "cold hand." For many years there was a kerosene lantern in the night fog, swinging along a path just like it would on the arm of someone walking. Then there are stories about how during overcast times shafts of sunlight or moonlight had the oddest way of penetrating the clouds and falling in brief bursts in sharp focus on the lighthouse. This phenomenon some connect to the general UFO sphere and say that the lighthouse was built on a spot that serves as some sort of a navigational system for alien craft. Some of those folks say the entire peninsula is part of that system.

I've heard some strange theories about such things, things about the use of the Earth's magnetic field by alien craft and about a system of power points that are nothing more than beacons and buoys for these crafts. In this way of thinking much human religion and the human experience of spirits, hauntings, and the paranormal come about through these devices controlled by aliens. The folks who think this way often believe that even human systems of measurement, geography, and mapping are manipulated by aliens. One of the things they point to is the fact that the peninsula lies right on the 45th parallel, the midway point between the North Pole and the equator. They claim that there is a belt of such phenomena along the 45th all around the world.

Of course you have subsets of people with all sorts of ideas, all manner of interpretations and claims about conspiracies and cover-ups. Some insist that the government knows about these things or is even behind them. But you can't really get the normal folks talking about what they've seen. They don't want to seem like loonies blabbering about this stuff. So all this is low key around here for the most part. But among peninsula people this stuff goes way back. Back to the first fruit orchards, back to the mission days, and back before the white man. Like rural people everywhere, we have our secrets. Sure it's strange, but the way I see it, this stuff hasn't killed anybody yet.

Phantom King
on Beaver Island

Great Lakes islands seem set apart in the legends and folk lore of the big inland waters. Some say that the isolation and quirky ethnic cultures of many of these islands are what makes them fertile territory for supernatural observations and rich storytelling traditions. Others say that life on a small island has its own peculiar energy and psychology, that they are like ships permanently at sail. Islands, no matter how long their geological records and human history, have a temporary feel to them. We know that many arose from the depths and that by gradual erosion or Atlantean catastrophe, most will return to those depths.

There is also the matter of who is drawn to islands, what they are leaving behind on the mainland, and how they hope to chart a new life on a speck of ground in a watery world. We have many impressions about such things that flow from our cultural imprints about pirates, lost civilizations, and white men "gone native." But those are archetypes of the seas, mostly the tropical seas at that. How might such imagery play out in the cold waters of the upper Great Lakes?

It was not until I met Neil in Charlevoix, Michigan, that I had much of an idea how strange things could get on a Great Lakes island. In my native Wisconsin I had heard a fair number of ghost stories and American Indian oral traditions on Lake Michigan's Washington Island and Lake Superior's Madeline Island. But such tales were either eerie or instructive on their own terms and did not frame bizarre political and social conditions. It was not until Neil educated me about his home island that I realized that those exotic locales of the warm seas had nothing on Beaver Island.

*　　*　　*

We've always been set apart on Beaver Island and which ever group came here they soon went a bit goofy. Just being on that island makes you think the rest of the world doesn't matter. Maybe just makes you wish everybody else would just stay away. I've heard that from every group that came, from my grandmother's Potawatomi and French ancestors to the employees of the American Fur Company to the rump Mormons to the Irish fishermen.

Now you could look at it one way, the view that the place drew cranks and crackpots. Or you could take the position that the island itself exerts a force on the human subconscious. Or maybe on the soul itself. If you take the first position you would think the original natives, not having a cultural heritage of eccentrics, would be an exception to the rule. But maybe they simply had a culture in which personality disorders are seen in spiritual terms. That sort of blurs the lines doesn't it? Maybe prophets are just a hop, skip, and a jump from being off their nut? Could be that Beaver Island is just the shovel that digs up this buried trait in people? Those are the type of ideas that come to you out on an island.

In our family the stories suggest that it is the island itself that changes the people. At least that is what was passed down from Potawatomi of mixed blood, who claimed that the lesser manitous made mischief here. And that is what we heard about the voyageurs who left their mark here, stories about the boasts and competitions that ended in fights. Finally, that is what was also remembered about the first American merchants, men who were not above letting the rivalry of commerce expand to the disappearance of competitors.

Then there were the Mormons, or at least rebel Mormons or a Mormon splinter group. You don't hear much of that breed up this way. Not many people know that they passed this way and left few traces. Just the stories of madness on Beaver Island.

It all started when this Mormon leader James Jesse Strang brought a group to the island in 1847. Right from the start he was kind of pushy and set up a more regimented framework than the mixed bloods, Frenchmen, and traders were accustomed to. It wouldn't have been so bad if it had been live and let live. But the Mormons had the numbers and soon outvoted everyone else and took over local government. That had the other locals in a lather, but the worst was yet to come.

Old Man Strang got stranger and stranger notions. He started taking orders from archangels and yelling at demons. He started communicating with the prior island inhabitants going back thousands of years. He became more alienated from the main Mormon hierarchy. He was given to staggering around the island in what was called a "holy ecstasy," delivering prophecy and commands from on high. All this from a fellow who didn't exhibit such symptoms prior to his island sojourn.

More and more Irish came to the area to practice the fishing trade and tensions grew. The Irish came to think of Strang as the Devil himself, finding his theology and personal behavior further beyond the pale than even the deviant Protestantism that parish priests had railed against back on the ould sod. Then Strang took the ultimate step that provoked the wrath of the Irish and which brought Strang to the attention of the federal government and foreign powers. The old bedbug declared himself King Strang and started to make enlarged claims of sovereignty.

Much of what went on was total fantasy in Strang's head, but he did have a bunch of followers who hung on his every word. His presumption extended to sending envoys to the Indian tribes and loose talk about annexing Canada. Apparently the British ambassador delivered a note to the U.S. government suggesting that King Strang be deposed or the British might feel free to launch a punitive expedition.

Things moved slow in those days, so there was no immediate action. But the Irish had little patience. The word "king" was filled with unhappy associations in their Gaelic circles. They were spoiling for a fight, and eventually King Strang provoked them with further usurpation of local government and its coffers. The result was the Battle of Pine River, a complete route of these quasi-Mormons in 1853.

While the talk of secession and independent empire was quashed, the Strang settlement continued to dominate the island. But Strang's habits and hearing of voices spread amongst his flock and they were soon wracked with dissension. Finally a splinter within the splinter revolted against Strang and assassinated him during the Coup of 1856. After that most of his followers slunk off into the sunset. A few stayed behind, took up normal life, and mostly kept their mouths shut about the whole sorry mess. Those would be among my ancestors.

One thing they did talk about in their dotage is seeing the phantom of Kind Strang. Yeh, that's one of the things that marks old age for males in my family, they start to see King Strang wandering around muttering in his longjohns, wearing a copper and brass crown. Not long after that they're usually muttering and walking around in their underwear themselves.

So that's what I have to look forward to. That's why I'm getting crankier and crankier. You're lucky you caught me in good mood, a talkative mood. Some days I'd just as soon see an end to the ferry. Just leave us out on Beaver Island wandering around, talking to the spirits and King Strang.

Part II
Down Huron
from Mackinac

Mackinac Rendezvous

*T*he straits connecting Lake Michigan to Lake Huron represent more than a change in bodies of water. Lake Michigan, after all, is exclusively the territory of the United States. Lake Huron is shared with our Canadian neighbors. In terms of legends and lore it also represents a shift in story, cadence, a seasoning of French origin, with the sounds of the metis patois.

Lake Huron's stories often have deeper roots than the tales of the other "Big Sisters." Many of the stories go back to the golden age of fur trading, some back to its very beginning. Mackinac Island is an excellent starting point for those old stories. It is the place where many of the customs and usages of fur trade began. It was the early crossroads that knitted the upper lakes together.

Many of my sources believed that Mackinac was one of the first places to experience the exuberant side of interactions between American Indians and French traders. The French had a generation or two to develop the ties and experience that gave rise to the intimacy that allows for celebration. An invitation to a tribal dance was likely the first step in a cultural exchange that progressed to French ballads, foot races, shooting contests, great feasts, and, eventually, alcoholic beverages.

What we are talking about are the antecedents of the rendezvous, that frontier gathering that reigned supreme for nearly two centuries under three flags. Rendezvous ghosts are fairly common from the forks of the Ohio to the headwaters of the Yellowstone and from Hudson Bay to bayou country. Rendezvous ghosts can be seen as a subset of what I call "rowdy ghosts." Howard, my informant on Mackinac Island, believes that "his ghosts" are set apart by the rendezvous rituals that were perfected on the island.

*   *   *

These eyes have seen the Rendezvous Ghosts. There are lessons to be learned in such things. Things from three hundred years ago that were not written down in the journals of gentlemen or priests.

Things that came together in this place and created different traditions and enduring differences in life around the Great Lakes. I really do believe that the classic Great Lakes rendezvous developed on Mackinac Island.

Those early years of French dominance of the trade were rough and tumble, with ten illegal traders for every one operating under license. The fur wars with the English had not begun, the Dutch had not yet armed the Iroquois to the teeth, and the Great Lakes area still teemed with furbearing animals. It was a beautiful interlude which generated many traditions that came to represent an entire subculture.

At the center of that subculture stood the *voyageur,* the sturdy and stocky laborer of the fur trade. When I see the ghosts it is the voyageurs that I mainly see. Not the flamboyant and eccentric voyageurs of the later Anglo-American era, but the simple peasant stock who fled oppressive conditions in Alsace and Lorraine or who sought out the New World to escape the semi-feudal life of Normandy and Brittany. They were not yet called voyageurs, just as these early gatherings were not yet called rendezvous. The names for such things came later.

In those early times, before the Jesuits insinuated themselves into every cranny of the fur network, the island went by its full name: *Michilimackinac.* It was a way station known to Hurons, Ojibiwe, Potawatomi, Ottawa, Sac, and Fox. The French explorers certainly stopped and sojourned here. But it was the independent-minded traders who followed who saw the commercial advantage of the island's location.

Now you're going to ask how I know these things since the historical record is sketchy concerning those times. The voyageurs left little in the way of written records. The state historical park focuses more on the British colonial period, not the French. And what little that is preserved about the French is about the military side of the Great Lakes heritage, the fur wars or the French and Indian Wars. But I get to see it and hear it myself. Yep, I can see the spirits of that time right among us on the island.

Mostly early summer is when I see and hear the long dead participants in rendezvous past. That was the time of rendezvous when the furs still came from around the Great Lakes. In later years the rendezvous moved westward to Lake Superior and up the Missouri River and were held later to account for the thousand mile trips from out of the heart of the continent. But here on Mackinac Island the rendezvous was a celebration of the brief warm season by those who had spent long winters of isolation and hard work.

The *hivernants,* those who overwintered in the back country, looked forward to the trip to Mackinac. They and their Indian wives would often journey weeks to get to Mackinac. Before they would paddle ashore they would change into their best clothes, groom themselves, and perhaps even bathe in the lake. This was the ultimate social occasion. This was usually their one trip out of the *pays d'en haut,* the up country of smaller lakes and flowages of Wisconsin, Minnesota, and Ontario. Often they came in the company of large parties of Indian inlaws and allies.

Here on Mackinac the division between different classes of voyageurs first became evident. The up country fur traders and trappers had the highest status at Mackinac rendezvous. Next came the long distance trade canoe crews who contracted for specific numbers of voyages and portages. Then came the once a year laborers brought out from the settled eastern villages of New France, the *engages,* who had been lured away from farms and workshops by the promise of adventure.

Those young men from the settlements were always surprised by what they saw here. While New France was never as race conscious as the English colonies, the men from the Montreal area were always surprised to see the extent to which the back country men had gone native. Many of the back country men had totally adopted Indian customs, dress, and even religion. It is those spirits of those hivernants who still linger on the island in great numbers.

A farm boy from along the Saint Lawrence would have grown up within the strictures of parish life. Here on Mackinac he would see white men offering the pipe to the Great Spirit. He would witness the men and women coming out of the sweat lodges naked and diving into the cold lake. He would hear the old voyageurs sing incredibly vile *chansons* while their audiences roared in laughter. He would usually stand apart at first, then be tempted by the wine offered by the fire. Finally he would join the dancing and perhaps find himself with a hivernant's metis daughter when he woke up with a bad headache.

You may think I'm crazy, but I'm not the only one who has seen or heard these voyageurs at large on the island. It's a talent to see such things. A talent that proves a quotient of Huron metis blood in one's veins. Hurons were a haunted people and they gave their name to this haunted lake. And truth be known, it was they who gave form to the early rendezvous, despite everything bad that happened to them. They befriended those voyageurs and mingled their blood with them despite political manipulation, war, disease, and brutal religious conversion.

It was not a pretty story here on the lakes. But it was a different story from the way it worked in most of the United States. Here the French way held sway, no removals or eradication pogroms. The Rendezvous Ghosts here show me a bond, an admission of intertwined histories and fates. This is what makes the spirits of the rendezvous different here than out on the Plains or in the Rockies. Those places are haunted by the swagger of proud frontiersmen who measured their manhood by the number of Indian scalps on their belt.

This is why we have tribes who managed to hang on around the lakes, even though removal was tried many times. Mackinac Island is a symbol of the other side of the tale of European and American Indian relations. It even has hints in it of what could have been, had not greed and lust for power won the day.

In the soft island twilight I watch the spirit revelers come into the clearings and gather around the fires. The words of friendship ring true. The exuberance of celebration is heartfelt. There is liberation in the whirl of the dance. Even in the drink there is fellowship and laughter, not the abuse that came later.

I feel it. I see it. I hear it. Some do. Some don't. Those who connect with it have a whole different relationship with Mackinac Island and Lake Huron. Those who don't connect with it are just passing through.

Witches of November

The good people of Mackinaw City treated me to many anecdotes and legends relating to the lakes. They helped fill in the blanks on the island-hopping that awaited me on the rest of my journey. The direct contacts they gave me would sustain me in stories all the way to Saginaw Bay.

These residents of Michigan's "north coast" have many unique angles on lake lore. They told me about weird waterfowl hunting rituals. They had endless tall tales about fishing. After one gray-haired wag told me about sailing a cast iron bathtub across Duncan Bay, a bushy bearded mountain of plaid had to top that with a story about his thirty-point buck that evaporated into spirit mist as he pulled the trigger.

The cafe contacts and barroom mentors of the area had me following up leads from Cheboygan to Alpena. And as pursuits of ghost stories go, there were the typical encounters with local eccentrics and folks with imbalances beyond my diagnostic capabilities. There were the usual story fragments and nonsequitors that posed riddles that the passage of time failed to unravel.

One odd lead about supernatural aspects concerning the weather made no sense at all. At first I chalked it up to the preoccupation that many lakeshore residents have with climate and the rigors thereof. Then, through those Mackinaw City contacts, I met Valentine, who brought new meaning to the word "cranky." He was cranky on the phone when I first called him, he was cranky as I walked up the weathered boardwalk to his cottage near Cordwood Point, and he was cranky as he walked me to my truck and gave me a cranky wave goodbye.

*   *   *

If you ain't gonna listen, you might as well get the hell out now. I ain't got time for stumblebums and halfwits who don't get it. Had a belly full of the likes of those breeds in my time, potlickers and outsiders who think they know squat! They don't know, cause they can't know. It's gotta be in the blood, you gotta be bred for it.

My people were of such a breed, wild Highlanders who also plied the North Sea. There lives no creature more filled to the brim with animal instinct and Neptune's eye than a Scot boatman. None! If you ain't gonna believe that, then you would do well to scratch your behind in someone else's home.

Make no mistake about it, a Scot boatman is a Scot boatman no matter he be transplanted to Nova Scotia, the Falklands, New Zealand, or bonny Lake Michigan. For that matter if he is warming his behind on the top floor of the Sears Tower. He can't help it, it's hereditary, like his hemorrhoids and his fondness for whiskey. The Grand Dad of my line often said it took ten generations of mating with English shepherdesses to breed the brine out of a Scot boatman. It must be so, for Grand Dad thumped his cane and his whiskey glass three times for the Trinity every time he uttered this pronouncement.

You gotta know our line if you're gonna understand the Witches of November. We stayed true to the blood even as the family moved into the wilds of North America. If half of the family tales are true — and Grand Dad's thumps of the cane and whiskey glass vouch for such a portion — then our clan clawed its way up the rivers of the American colonies three hundred years ago and by two hundred years were already on the Great Lakes. This is a legacy of men who kept an eye on the sky, one hand on the tiller, and the other hand free to snatch up a Kentucky rifle. Men who could read the prophecy made in the margins where sky, earth, and water meet and sometimes collide.

Such is my breed. A line of lake masters, fishermen, and veterans of the U.S. Navy. I did my twenty years of service, from a seaman boatswain taking Marines into Korea to a chief petty officer with my own riverboat in the brown water fleet in Vietnam. And in between those bookends of my time in Uncle Sam's Navy came the pleasure cruises to Iceland, the Aleutians, and Antarctica. Plenty of places to watch the wind and waves.

But it all started for me back with Grand Dad out on Bois Blanc Island. That is where he taught me to read the signs of weather and know the tricks of the spirits that move the elements. Bois Blanc was our summer training ground, and Grand Dad was headmaster, commandant, and Captain Bligh rolled into one. The old grizzled veteran of Navy landing parties during the Boxer Rebellion and of Admiral Dewey's excursion into Manila Bay had charge of me in those times when Dad was sailing the saltwater on merchant ships. Bois Blanc is where you could learn the signs and listen to those spirits.

I was a boy when Grand Dad first told me about the Witches of November. I was ten years old when he told me that they were different from the November Witches, the latter being the common name for the violent storms so common in November. He said the Witches of November he talked about were real witches, spirit women who could manipulate weather. He said they were a coven of old hags who had plagued Scot boatmen from the Orkneys to the Bering Strait. And he said that Bois Blanc was one of their favorite places to brew up storms.

Even at 10, a boy's gonna be a bit skeptical of such a charge. Especially he made without the sacred oath of thumping cane and glass. But as if to offer proof Grand Dad made arrangements to take me to Bois Blanc in early November of 1940 for a little outing. Dad was already running supplies to England and dodging U-boats. Grand Dad packed a large larder and all manner of gear making me wonder if we would winter on the island.

Once installed in our cozy encampment, Grand Dad started weaving tales and experiences in a mixture so rich and intoxicating that my ten year old brain might as well have been sharing his whiskey. He told me about the witches and how they stirred their evil cauldron out on the Witch's Finger, his name for a point on the north side of Bois Blanc. He told me about the wiles of women in tones I didn't fully understand until I lounged in the velvet parlors of Kowloon. He even provided me instructions for the eventuality that I would not find a Scotswoman for a mate. He said to find a fallen Irish Catholic woman, one with foul words on her tongue for priests and other shearers of flocks. And he told me about the Freshwater Fury of 1913.

This was known as the Great Storm of the time just before the Great War. Grand Dad survived an ore boat breakup on the terrible night of November 8, 1913, and made it ashore in Ontario. He said the toll of that night was almost 300 dead, eight ships sunk, and more than fifty ships damaged. There were winds of sixty to eighty miles per hour and seas of over forty feet.

All the while Grand Dad is telling me this, lulling me with stories in our cozy shelter, the wind is coming up outside. We felt it shift late in the day of November 10, 1940. Grand Dad gave a knowing look at the sky and thumped his walking stick on a rock. Then on November 11, 1940, *She* came. Grand Dad spoke that Armistice Day of all the veterans of our clan, from the Highland wars for independence to French and Indian and the Spanish-American. As he spoke the sky howled and freezing rain and then snow pelted our lean-to. When we peeked out the sight terrified me. I thought the waves would wash right over the island.

Grand Dad had planned well and we weathered that night. A boy learned many lessons about watching sky, earth, and water. So much so that many a Navy aerographer's mate would ask me to take a look topside. The Armistice Day storm took fifty-nine lake sailors and twenty or so people on the islands and mainland. But we were not among the casualties, for Grand Dad knew the signs and the charms against the witches' brew.

You gotta understand the old Highland signs in such times. You must know how the witches practice their dark trade. The timing is the main thing! Think of the season, man! It's the time of All Hallows Eve and All Saints Day, the time for things unnatural to be out and about. The old ones in the Highlands called it Sowen, the great autumn feast marking the approach of winter. Their tricks and magic in that fragile season can bring quick changes.

That's the thing about these storms sent by the Witches of November. Quick changes. Violent changes. The worst ones seem to follow unseasonably mild weather. That's how it was in 1940. Barely needed a jacket when we headed to Bois Blanc. Within forty-eight hours a parka and long johns were barely enough. That's why some duck hunters froze sitting in their john boats that day.

Grand Dad told me that day that I would be under the spell for those witches for the rest of my life. He said they were the breed that made hard men hard and he counted himself in the happy company of those who stiffened their resolve after witchly ministration. He even said they made damn fine wives for Scot boatmen if a man had the pocket stones to handle one. I don't know exactly what he meant by that, but he thumped the stick thricely and gave me my first whiskey.

Sloop of the Radiant Boy

Ghost stories abound in the stretch of Michigan between the Straits of Mackinac and Saginaw Bay. Surprisingly, many, if not most, have no relation to lake themes. One can find traditional haunted houses in Rogers City, Hagensville, Cathro, Spruce, Harrisville, and Alabaster. Presque Isle is alleged to have an abandoned pioneer cemetery where the spirits dance quite spritely come All Hallows Eve. Greenbush is said to be home to a ghost blacksmith. Au Sable may be the home base of a phantom woodsman who roams the Huron National Forest.

What is interesting about many of these story fragments in this area is their European antecedents. Like the Highland flavor in the story of the Witches of November of Bois Blanc, many of these coastal ghost tales are filled with old country archetypes. Unlike much of Upper Great Lakes territory, one finds little evidence of the story influence of the original inhabitants here. Where there is mention of the Huron, Ottawa, or Potawatomi peoples, it is incidental to narratives that first evolved in Northern Europe.

One such European story tradition did have a lake connection. In much of the British Isles, the Low Countries, and maritime Germany there were apparitions known as luminous children, though one hears less of such phenomena today. This is a ghostly species that arises through horrible circumstances. The one found in the Alpena, Michigan vicinity was the first clear example of this type that I encountered in North America.

Wallace has the roots to tell the tale. The story tumbled out of him during a walk southward along the shore of Thunder Bay. The regret and sadness in his voice soon informed me that this was a story that touched his heart.

*   *   *

While I was growing up we called him the Radiant Boy. What is it, five, six decades since I first heard the story after seeing the strangest thing? I was out fishing with Uncle Marlin, the catch was good and the sun went down on us. I was tired and rested my head for a moment while Uncle Marlin pulled up the anchor rope. I heard a change in the sound of the water, not the lapping on our boat, but the cutting sound of a sailing craft slicing through the low swells.

The sound made me jerk my head up. A sloop swooshed by less than ten yards away, without so much as a creak of line or snap of sail. It startled me and I almost tumbled overboard. I had not noticed it and my uncle was turned in the opposite direction. But the real surprise came as I did a doubletake and looked at the passing stern. There stood a short human figure and in the dark it looked like he was illuminated by an inner glow. He had such a pained expression.

I yelled to my uncle and he looked up. He saw nothing because it had slipped away in the darkness. When I told Uncle Marlin what I had seen I could hear the old man take a deep breath in the dark. He didn't say anything for several minutes as he coiled the last few yards of rope and tidied up our equipment. Then he lit his pipe with three matches at once. I could see his eyes in the match glare and they were very moist with tears.

"Young fellow, that's the Radiant Boy," he said with a tone of pure grief. He went on to explain that I had just seen a ghost, a very unusual ghost with very unusual history. I didn't know the half of it at the time. There was lots to learn about this type of ghost.

It turns out that my family has a historic connection to this whole thing. My ancestors are from Cumberland in England. It turns out that that region of the British Isles was a hotbed of glowing ghosts of children. It seems that there is one such famous ghost at Corby Castle. But there are others of more common origin representing almost every era from the time of the plagues to the witch persecutions to the sweatshops of the Dickens' era to the World War II air raids.

The farthest back I could find any English report of glowing spirit children was in the 9th Century. That's when the Saxons started raiding and settling the British Isles in a serious way. The Saxons knew of Baltic stories of glowing ghosts of children. Such stories went back to ancient tribal times and may have an origin in ritual infanticide.

That's usually the key element in these glowing children, the element of murder by a parent. So according to legend the mere appearance of such a ghost was usually evidence of foul deeds that were often concealed. I've even read that the presence of luminous youthful spirits was used to condemn witches suspected of sacrificing children to the devil. There was also a martyrdom aspect to this, with the ghosts of rebellious children who wished to go on crusades acting as guardian spirits to pious knights and pilgrims.

There is so much lore about glowing ghosts of children that I can't remember it all. Some of the significant parts are glowing ghosts as omens. If you see a glowing child and he draws his forefinger across his throat in the universal sign of death then that is an omen of impending doom. If you see a glowing child and she is rocking a cradle then that is a omen of pregnancy and birth. Some glowing children act as guides, leading lost people home though fog or snow.

Our Radiant Boy is a breed apart. First, it is the only one I know of that occurs on water and on a sailing vessel. In this case a fore-and-aft rigged boat with one mast and a single headsail jib. It is also the only one I know of that has a name connected to the ghost, in this case "Michael." Some people call him that and link it to an early Michigan family. Others say wait a minute and claim that the name is really the name of the sloop. Uncle Marlin always said that the sloop was named after the boy.

I had to talk to many people to piece together the full story of Michael. With each old widow and lake codger came another little bit of the story. Some were embellished a little with the source's family angle. Isn't it always that way with a story? Almost everyone I talked to felt like they were grieving for the child. Some would break down during the telling of their accounts and were unable to continue. Always the story came back to the sadness over the circumstances of Michael's death. It seems that his mother killed him, perhaps accidentally, but in any event caused him to fall while she was in a fit of rage.

There is something about these circumstances that touches and horrifies people. Something unnatural about the one who gives a child life being the one who takes that life. It is as if some basic rule of the universe has been broken and all civilized conduct is brought into doubt. It raises our fear and fuels insecurity. No matter how tranquil the time and place, such a crime reminds us that evil and psychosis lurk close to the surface. Maybe it also reminds people of some inner rage that they keep under wraps and makes then worry about losing control. Maybe it reminds them of the brutal and unkind things in their own childhood.

Our Radiant Boy supposedly loved the lake and loved being out on the sloop with his father. His mother wanted to protect young

Michael and make a gentleman out of him. She wanted a future for him beyond that of a self-employed sloop master running as a packet down to Port Huron or as a ferry across Thunder Bay. But he was a defiant child and would often slip away to the boat against her wishes. One early morning she caught him at the top of the stairs sneaking out of their home in Alpena. Did she grab at him or push him? The result was the same; the boy tumbled and broke his neck. It's said that the father was so heartbroken that he sailed away on the sloop and was never seen again.

But the sloop was seen, at least in ghostly form. It was seen all over Thunder Bay, or as the lakemen call it, "Little Thunder Bay." Sightings were common at South Point down by Negwegon State Park. The sloop was seen from the mouth of the Pine River at Oscoda up to Crooked Island. Michael's mother heard about these reports, but didn't believe them. That is she didn't believe them until she saw a fog lift off Thunder Bay right off Alpena and was confronted with the misty image of the sloop standing off a mere fifty yards.

She was the first one to see the glowing ghost of her son in the stern of the sloop. She was the one to first utter the words "Radiant Boy." Was the term acknowledgment of the historic Cumberland roots or a personal endearment between mother and son? We'll never know, for the mother went mad soon after that and was beyond communication. In less than a year she was found drowned near the spot where the sloop moored when it was still a vessel for the living.

Nymphs on Saginaw Bay

S ometimes when one is on the trail of a ghost story it turns out to be something other than what is suggested by reports. Ghosts become a catchall for all manner of odd happenings. Sources bring an assortment of quirks and personal perceptions to their encounters with the paranormal. Such people will talk of hauntings, but it is often they who are haunted by things that do not fit neatly into the normal vocabulary.

In part this is because we modern types have lost our pre-industrial cosmology. Pre-industrial peoples would find much of our talk of ghosts shallow and one-dimensional. Those who process their world views according to Earth-focused belief systems usually see supernatural events within a context of spirit presences within all natural systems, not just as manifestations of departed souls. The term "ghosts" does not fit all of these circumstances or occurrences.

Additional reports of female presences out on Lake Huron islands made me think that the witches of Bois Blanc were more widespread than initially thought. Soon I found that these reports covered a multitude of observations and claims that did not fit any pattern. Most were dead ends, pure and simple. Others were humorous tall tales trotted out for my entertainment. One old lake boatman warned me that wags were sending me on mermaid hunts, the Great Lakes equivalent of the Southern snipe hunt.

All the other leads had been exhausted when I stopped in the Museum of the Great Lakes in Bay City, Michigan. No one there knew much about these stories but they did refer me to a contact. When I called Sheridan he was a little reluctant to talk. He finally agreed to meet me at a bench along the Saginaw River. His jitters told me this would be a different sort of tale.

* * *

I don't know what to think. I've had some problems. Had to take medication for awhile. But they say I'm okay now. The doctor told me I went through some sort of trauma. Darn if I know what it was though. You know shrinks. They think everything goes back to the time you saw your mother in a leather harness.

When did I first see the girls of the lake? I think it was in the 1960s as a boy. But I didn't realize then what it was that I was seeing. It wasn't until I was older that I realized that not everyone could see them. But I'm not the only one who sees them, so I'm not totally crazy. I've found over the years that it is often children that see them and sometimes old men.

Our family had a tradition of casual pleasure boating, so we were on the lake with some regularity. I don't go out anymore, my doctor thinks it causes me stress and sets off episodes. But when I was a teenager we would sometimes motorboat out to Charity Island. I would walk while the others paired off in couples. That's when I became aware of seeing the girls of the lake. That's when I first realized this was something out of the ordinary.

I tried to talk about it around the campfire, but the others laughed at me. Some said I was seeing the ghosts of some girls who had drowned on the lake. They hooted about my ghost girlfriends and on one of our little excursions, they planted one of those inflatable party dolls on the beach. They called the doll my date and forced me to lug it around. If I hadn't, they would have left me behind. It was a miserable time in my life.

Later I started to see the girls of the lake when I was by myself, which I started to prefer over the company of taunters, jokesters, and bullies. Usually it was a group of three, but sometimes it was one particular girl. It must confess I started to become quite infatuated with her. I started to fantasize about her and actively search for her. I would watch her from hidden spots. It would just ruin my day if I couldn't find her.

An old man once caught me spying. I thought he would ridicule me, too, but instead he educated me about what I was seeing. He said he had been watching the girls since he was a young man and that they had been around for a long time before that. So right away I thought this confirmed the ghost angle. But he set me straight and let me know there was more to it than that.

He called them "nymphs." It was the first time I ever heard that word. He told me about a whole tradition of young beauties who dwell by large bodies of water and delight in messing with young men's minds. Apparently they cause no harm except to the rare male who becomes obsessed and loses self-control. Maybe I'm on the cusp of that. If so, I'd say that the old-timer who filled me in was right off the deep end. That geezer had a very unwholesome attitude about the girls. I mean to tell you, he would talk about things that were against the law in Michigan.

It turns out nymphs are noted for beauty and are invariably un-clothed. That limits their presence to our short warm season. The old fellow said it was always that way, just the summer months and that occasional summer-like September we get here. And he said it was always the same story of mischief and seduction.

Another time he was filling me in on things he had done with the nymphs. It sounded more like fantasy to me. Anyway, his wife started hovering around and he shifted gears. He started talking about nymphs as an insect hatch and as a type of hand-tied fly for fishing. His wife seemed real suspicious.

He had studied such creatures and the ways they appeared in other places around the world. He said that humans had always had problems classifying these things. Most places they were con-sidered half-spirit, half-human. He believed that they went through a cycle that was sort of like mortal life, a long period of appearance in the flesh during which they could physically interact with hu-mans. After a long time, centuries or more, they lose their vital force and become more a phenomenon of sight and sound.

He was filled with nostalgia for romps with these girls of the lakes. Their sweet voices, their laughter like bubbling water, and their dances on the beaches were all part of his memories. He said our nymphs had the long custom of welcoming the summer solstice with a bonfire and midnight dance on the sand. I never saw that, but it did seem like they were particularly active around that time.

The old fellow debunked the idea that the nymphs were of re-cent origin, off of Greek freighters or such. Since he had some Scan-dinavian blood in him he was convinced that they were of Nordic origin. They certainly have the stature, physique, and color of skin, hair, and eyes to support that theory. This view would have them as stowaways and camp followers on those ancient Viking expedi-tions to North America.

The old fellow also gave me his formula for holding power over a nymph. He said an old Roma, you know, a Gypsy, told him how to do it. Apparently you soak three wrought iron nails in the water at the beach the nymph uses. You leave the nails underwater from new moon to new moon. Then you nail them into a piece of drift-wood. You place it on the beach and bait the trap with something shiny like jewelry. When she touches the shiny object on the drift-wood she is then under a spell. The spell lasts until the driftwood with nails is returned to the lake.

I know you're thinking that this is some sort of delusion for dirty old men with a fixation on sweet young things. Or maybe a mental disorder peculiar to little Walter Mittys who have otherwise empty lives. My doctor says it is a variation on the Lolita theme and that it has afflicted grown men for ages, makes them addled and vulnerable. I don't know how that fits for me, I've been hooked since I was a boy.

I find it sad if the old man is right, that the nymphs are fading away and are now just ghosts of the vital creatures they once were. It makes me sad personally, that's true. But it makes me sad for us all if we live in a time when beauty, vigor, and freedom are fading. We need those qualities in tangible form, not as apparitions.

The Bird Lady
of Burnt Cabin Point

Explorations of Michigan's thumb took me on many of the back roads of Huron County. Hints of old legends and lore abound in this region. The place names themselves suggest stories: Grind Stone City, Bad Axe, Port Hope, Kilmanagh, and Burnt Cabin Point. Area historic sites like Pioneer Huron City and Sanilac near New Greenleaf also tease visitors with echoes of the past. All these places produced leads to fine specimens of local folktales. Alas, there was little in the way of supernatural content among them.

It was only on my second visit to the Burnt Cabin Point area that I was able to generate a solid lead in a ghost story. A woman on a walk with a golden retriever disabused me on any notion of hauntings arising out of the conflagration that give Burnt Cabin Point its name. But she did allow that the point area had its hauntings, especially in the form of an eccentric old lady of comparatively recent origin. She disclaimed knowledge of the specifics and instead sent me down the lakeshore road that forms a loop off Highway 25 out on the point. She gave me directions to her aunt's modest Cape Cod-style home.

Katherine greeted me warmly at the door in a way that made me suspect that her niece had a mobile phone in her fanny pack. Her name fit her well as she bore some resemblance to Katharine Hepburn without the New England accent. She had me bring the tray of lemonade out on a deck behind the house where a little garden enclosure bristled with bird feeders and all manner of feathered friend paraphernalia. It was a perfect setting for her account of her favorite ghost.

*   *   *

Welcome, welcome, my good man. Isn't it a lovely day? A day to chirp out our good fortune at being alive. A day for the soul to soar and for the voice to take flight.

So it's ghosts that interest you and stories that entertain you. I've heard such tales in my time, but they're more like rumors and allegations. Most of them don't have meat on the bones. As for me, my own direct experience is meager, my ghostly encounters rather limited. To be honest, and precise in the measure, I have a ghost story repertoire of exactly one story. Only one that I am qualified to speak of in any detail based on personal acquaintance.

The only spirit presence that has seen fit to reveal its existence to me is our Bird Lady. If you ask around you may find a few individuals up in years who knew her while she lived out here. But I doubt if any will admit that her spirit is still among us or offer to tell you what our Bird Lady is up to.

She lived from the 1880s to the 1950s, with her prime coming in the time of the Great Depression and World War II. She was a lot of things that were uncommon for a woman in those days. She lived alone and was pretty much self-sufficient. She was a self-educated naturalist and conservationist, she loved to quote Muir and Thoreau. I believe she corresponded with Aldo Leopold and Gifford Pinchot. She knew how to splint a bird's wing and rehabilitate it and how to build a fish trap.

The Bird Lady earned her name for the things she did for birds, especially lake birds. She recognized before others did that humans were changing the habitat and destroying the connection between all the species that depend on water and wetlands. Some recall that she seemed like a magnet for birds. Her old shack seemed more like a roost. The old-timers in the area said she could walk up to birds and touch them. She had power over birds. And maybe she drew some power from birds.

Some odd stories were told about the Bird Lady during her lifetime. Things about her ability to use birds to make charms and spells. Those things were said mainly by those inclined toward suspicion and jealousy. She certainly had her detractors, the usual kind who are intolerant of those outside the mainstream. They didn't really move against her; they were scared of her.

Such fear continued for that generation even after she died. It was said she was seen as an apparition wherever there were gatherings of shore birds. Some think that wherever and whenever a bird does something strange that the spirit of the Bird Lady is part of the explanation. While that covers a multitude of improbable circumstances, there may be a kernel of truth here. There are some things involving birds that seem to have her signature on them.

You must understand how the Bird Lady viewed birds and the imprint she left with some of us. She knew that birds were more than mere feathered creatures. She explained the Irish lore about sea gulls embodying the souls of drowning victims. She let us know that a black bird over water, especially a crow or raven, is a harbinger of death. She taught us that a land bird flying into the cabin of a vessel tells us that news or a message will soon follow. She spread the knowledge that a seabird far from water can be a message from someone traveling abroad.

She could also break it down bird by bird. Ospreys were the carriers of souls, especially the souls of those spiritually attuned. Eagles are always an auspicious sign, conferring blessings and strength. Eagles flying from east to west were a particularly good sign. A dawn flight of geese signals a major arrival, while a dusk flight of geese signals a surprise departure. Owls along the coast or, worse yet, perched in a tree over a significant body of water, are a very bad omen. On the other hand, an owl hooting in a boathouse or dock shed is viewed as good luck, as is a tree used by shipwrights which had an owl's nest hole in it.

Some of these things lead to the forms of augury she talked about. Augurs were originally those who interpreted bird signs. Auspices were originally the set of meanings derived from birds signs by augurs. Both words derive from *avis specio,* which means birdwatching. Some of the main auspices were a vulture eating a dead owl, a crow eating dead waterfowl, a waterfowl on a house roof, a seagull on a tombstone, and so forth. Then there were more sophisticated forms of augury involving looking at bird entrails.

She didn't forget about the birds of the other realms, the ones that inhibit other levels of existence. She was convinced that birds in regular dreams usually represented angels. Birds seen in trances and altered states represented supernatural assistance, escape, and the perspective of great height. The mythological birds were said to actually dwell in other worlds accessible to those possessing the ancient secrets of travel to those places.

For her these birds of the other realms had a strong connection to the beliefs of the ancient peoples. This was tied to most of the old religions and explains much religious symbolism, everything from the "Ba" of the ancient Egyptians, which rose out of the body as a bird form of the soul, to the Christian dove. Name the group, she could tell you how birds fit into their theology and psychology. She knew it all from Viking Valhalla to the Thunderbird of the American Southwest.

The Bird Lady died in an autumn of strange bird sightings. After she died the weird sightings continued. All this combined in the minds of those who didn't like her to support their whispers of powers of the dark side. This is why some will say that the Bird Lady was capable of taking bird form herself to spy on and interfere with the lives other others.

I don't discount that possibility, even with her long dead. Too many things have happened that point to her presence here among us. What would you call it if an oriole joins you on your hammock? Or if a rare Kirtland's warbler sits on your glass of lemonade and takes a sip? Wouldn't you wonder if those were things you saw her do when she was living?

The Bird Lady has no sinister agenda. There's no horror in any of this. She's just enjoying the freedom of her status as a feathered friend. So I try to make sure she feels welcome here. That's why I take care of all the birds that come here. You never know which one might turn out to be her. I guess I'm in training to be the next bird lady.

Port Huron Vigil

ometimes it is hard to tell just how a ghost has come to haunt
a place. Sometimes the circumstances that underlie the haunt
ing are obscure or shrouded in the mists of the past. Sometimes the Great Lakes origins of a ghost may be lost as time changes
both the landmarks and the cultural reverence points. So I learned
on my circumnavigation of the upper Great Lakes. More than once
during this journey I found that a haunted dock of long ago had
given way in succession to tons of fill, warehouses, and, eventually,
condominiums.

Port Huron offered a fair amount of spirit lore, which at first
blush seemed disconnected from things of the lakes. The community has its share of cemetery ghosts, pantry poltergeists, and old
Victorian haunted houses. Still, Port Huron is more about faculty
dinners, small tidy galleries, and cozy restaurants than it is about
gothic sensibilities and eerie happenings.

*Many, if not most, sources for ghost stories are well rooted in their
communities and well acquainted with local history. Many are up in
years and are witnesses, if not participants, in that history. Occasionally,
a newcomer has a spirit encounter that sparks their sense of mystery and
their interest in local heritage. So it was with Len, who moved to Port
Huron years ago to open an antique business and as part of the bargain
found a little piece of haunted history.*

* * *

Shortly after I moved and set up shop I found myself at the old
port district, near the bridge, to give an estimate on some estate
items in storage in an old two story brick building. Before the place
was renovated it had a second story bay window that afforded a
view of the lake and the St. Clair River. In the course of looking
over the junk that passed for heirlooms, the caretaker told me the
building had passed through stages as a lake freight office, a shippers' association branch, and as a reporting station. I had a rough
idea about what the first two functions might entail, but the third
activity escaped my understanding.

Just before I left the building the caretaker and I were standing beneath that large window and I happened to look up. What I saw was so fleeting that initially I thought my eyes were playing tricks on me. A dark human figure was standing close to the window, with face nearly pressed to the glass panes. It was a quick view of someone looking out toward the lake. Just as quickly the figure was gone.

The caretaker saw my quizzical look and looked up also. He gently shook his head and murmured, "That's our Watcher." At first I thought he meant it was a watchman on rounds through the building. Then he explained that it was a ghost, a particular type called a "Watcher." He tried to explain what that meant and offered up all sorts of explanations about the origin of this ghost. He was off-base with most of his background.

This was my first ghost sighting ever, so I spent quite a bit of time trying to flesh it out from the caretaker's basic story. He mumbled something about a family business with a hovering and suspicious patriarch. He even tied the whole thing to a late delivery that the ghost was waiting for and watching for up at the big windows. And he threw in something about waiting for the return of lost love for good measure.

A bit of research proved to me that while the caretaker was in the ballpark with the generalities concerning Watchers, he was off by a mile on the specifics of this Watcher. It seemed odd to my friends that I, Mister Show-me-the-facts, would embrace the whole world of the paranormal after one shadowy glimpse at a window. But I certainly did. I found myself drawn to understand this phantom standing vigil. It did indeed take some detective work. Roger, my housemate, started his annoying habit of calling me "Nancy Drew." I soon found that I needed to understand not only the habits of ghosts, but also the history of maritime activity on the Great Lakes.

The caretaker was right about the general behavior and motivation of Watchers. This type of ghost is not interactive and seems to pay no heed to the living. It is frequently found at old fortifications, such as castles in Europe. But the type pops up everywhere from widow's walks to railroad signal towers. Interestingly, there is a subset of Watchers connected to the world of ships and sailing, those who inhabit lighthouses and the wheelhouses and bridges of older vessels.

What I learned from my investigation is that our modern minds have trouble grasping all the conditions and subtleties of the past. That's why the caretaker and others had the reasons for our Watcher's vigil all turned around. You really need to know how shipping was administered and monitored years ago. You have to understand that Great Lakes ships were late in adopting radio technology. It was this lack of technology that clued me in to a whole realm of old time shipping activity that I had no idea existed prior to seeing the Watcher.

Do you have any idea what a reporting station is? Did you know that there was once a complex system of agents, clerks, and observers that kept a watchful eye on all passing vessels? Isn't it something that a vessel's movements could be charted by reconstructing the ship's logs of passing vessels, the observation notes of weather observers, the records of port-of-entry officials, the reports of Coast Guard patrols, and the dispatches of shipping agents? But that's how it was done on the Great Lakes from the time of the Civil War to the eve of World War II.

The system served several proposes. Safety was the foremost motivation. Crude as the reporting system was, it provided a way of directing salvage and rescue vessels to the scene of calamities. It also allowed for updates from searches and the charting of floating wreckage. Everyone connected to the lakes, from the lowliest net hauler to the superintendent of the big shipping lines, felt an obligation to keep their eyes peeled. The other considerations were chiefly business ones. A good reporting system allowed shipping companies to time dock work, ship reprovisioning, light repairs, and all other things that went along with the loading and unloading processes. A vessel passing Mackinac at such and such a time was the considered "due" in Port Huron or Green Bay in an approximate number of hours that could be adjusted for weather and other conditions.

Reporting stations varied considerably in their level of sophistication and resources. The system seemed to evolve over time from a hodge-podge of informal commercial and governmental observations to a network more or less under the control of lake shippers associations. In some places this meant a clerk with other duties bicycling off to a telegraph office to send a message. In other places there were on-premises communications including, ironically, the very radio technology that many shipowners neglected to install on their vessels.

So I believe that our Watcher ghost was a watcher by trade during his life. The connection was the building and the objects in it. That still left the question of what he was watching for that held him here in Port Huron on his decades long vigil? The answer to that is much more a matter of conjecture, but I have a theory based on ship artifacts I found in the building and later purchased from the estate.

It seems there was once a controversy about whether the Port Huron reporting station improperly reported a ship called the *Clifton* back in September of 1924. It appears that the *Clifton* went missing with all hands up in the middle of Lake Huron. What is lost to time is whether a report, if any, was filed erroneously on another vessel or whether someone at Port Huron saw a phantom *Clifton* pass into the St. Clair River. Storms that night threw off shipping timetables and it was fully a day before it was noted that the ship never made it to its Detroit destination.

This old whaleback freighter, a cigar-shaped design that made it look somewhat like a submarine running on the surface, was hauling stone out of Sturgeon Bay. It was seen clearly at the Mackinac reporting station. It was seen belching its usual black smoke off Forty Mile Point. It was seen by another vessel around midday, and the log of the other vessel noted that despite the storm that the *Clifton* was making way without difficulty. After that there is no reporting record.

When the search began it involved dozens of private vessels and the Coast Guard. Rumors of wreckage were heard from Presque Isle to the Bruce Peninsula in Ontario. Even the Army Air Corps got into the act with search planes launched from Selfridge Field. But it was another ship that found all that was left of the *Clifton*, a section of the pilothouse. In the pilothouse were items that established its provenance, a clock, a light beacon, and a chart holder.

The clock was a wheelhouse model of the Seth Thomas maritime clock. A fine piece of workmanship. The clock was stuck at one minute to midnight when I found it there in the building among the estate items. It is restored to working order now.

But things have changed. The Watcher is seldom seen on his Port Huron vigil anymore. The old building got a make-over and is now enjoying a new lease on life. Still, I think I may be the one who altered the cycle for our Watcher. It could be that repair of the clock did that. It unstuck time as it were. That's the tricky thing about antiques, restoration can cross over into change.

Part III
Georgian Bay
and North Passage

Kettle Point Lights

It is natural to assume that reference to a "light" on the lakeshore would have something to do with a lighthouse. Next to the vessels that ply the waters, lighthouses are the most common story motif of the Great Lakes and loom large as haunted environments. The assumption is usually valid as far as it goes, but sometimes one misses the nuances of a lead. Such was the result of the misimpression gained in conversation on the docks of Sarnia.

Busy workers and vendors couldn't be bothered with long conversations. The best they could do was to throw verbal clues over their shoulders. One common refrain had to do with the Kettle Point Lights. This, of course, raised the possibility of more than one lighthouse and more than one lighthouse story. It felt like I had hit the double jackpot with my first Canadian story.

It didn't turn out that way at all. Up at Kettle Point I found no one with any knowledge about haunted lighthouses. The Canadians who I asked kept kind looks on their faces that did not totally mask their feelings about strangers asking strange questions. Many of the locals were taciturn of demeanor and monosyllabic in response. The affirmative and negative grunts were positively enlightening compared to the noncommittal "hmms," and "hrumps," and "huhs."

Dawson overheard my fruitless inquiries at a counter where the only hot leads brought coffee or tea in mugs. His eyes lit up in a way that made clear his enjoyment of my futile questioning. He was content to let me suffer awhile longer before he eased my pain.

* * *

You Yanks are pretty ingenious about everything except people. You wouldn't drill your well by starting on a big rock pile? One wouldn't fire up the rig without putting in the bit? One wouldn't pound down through sand unless you brought some casing? Of course not! But this old Scot hole digger can tell you that's what you're doing if you're asking about ghosts and lighthouses here in Point.

A few of us know about the Kettle Point Lights, but they have absolutely nothing to do with lighthouses and their connection to ghosts is unclear at best. Not everything strange is a ghost. Even where you might have spirits at work it doesn't necessarily mean that the thing you see is the spirit itself. The flash and the bang are not the gunpowder, you know.

This is all about light, the flash as it were. What causes the light is an entirely different matter and the answers do not go much further than speculation. When I mention light I use the word on every level. There is the brightness to the thing and its side effects. Those who see it, and our numbers are not overly large, feel something with the light. It is more than something visual and optical. There is illumination in different ways. Some who see it come away feeling they know something more, something that they cannot quite put into words. Some even sense something divine in all this, something of the Light and of enlightenment.

When I have seen it the feeling was there. Maybe not on the level of [...] the epiphany o[...] belief or vision of a mystic. More just a w[...] accepting [...] good cheer and goodwill. One could s[...] equivalent of [...] a hot toddy or two in front of a blazing [...] there's a[...] connection there. After all, what [...] the to[ddy...] the fireplace other than vessels for the light [...]

As y[ou ...] around the lak[...]kes you will find that Kettle Point [...] not the [... places ...] happens[...]ns. I have heard stories of such [...] Soo[... the west] reaches of Superior, in the Upper Peninsula [... Michigan ... near] Marquette. I have even been to Watersmeet in the Upper Penin[sula...]la. That's the hot spot and per[...] even the very center of [...] things of this type. I saw the Watersmeet Lights [...] more in a seve[...]nty-two hour visit than I've seen the Kettle Point lights in a lifetim[...]e. Things Canadian are always a [...] was far less extravagant.

Naturally one has the issue of [...] he physical causes of such lights. I happen to think such things are linked by the underlying geological strata and related geomagnetism. We have atypical ore bodies in the area and some evidence of underwater petroleum. So perhaps the answers lie underground, and a drilled hole might yield the answers.

Then there are the explanations of legends and folklore. I once heard an old story about lights that lured a ship too close to shore where it broke up in storm waves. Supposedly there were some local scoundrels who robbed the survivors, maybe even murdered them. One can see where a story like that might be suppressed by the decent people who came later. It is hard to tell, though, because stories of light luring ships ashore to their doom are common within legends. One never knows.

This part of the tale is so close to the legend of the *Palatine* that one must wonder if the story was imported by those familiar with that older tragedy. It is my observation that stories are often shaped that way; patterns and themes find their way to distant locations when an explanation is needed for a strange occurrence.

But it is worth revisiting the *Palatine* story just to see if it brings any understanding of how lights might figure in this. There you had 18th Century German immigrants on a ship off North America's coast. Light lured them close to rocks, and the crew abandoned them. After that the story varies. Some say the ship went to the bottom. Others say that some rather nasty coastal residents came out to rob the passengers, loot the ship, and then burned the *Palatine.* That was a common ploy of the breed of scoundrels known as "land pirates." Thereafter the forlorn ship itself was ofttimes seen as a ghost and a glowing ghost ship at that. From light to light as it were.

One of the commonalities between that saltwater tale and our freshwater reports is the weather factor. Both traditions seem to include harbingers of abrupt weather changes and the arrival of severe storms. The local correlation between the lights and bad weather has been noted by a handful attuned to lake moods. Even so there may be some higher frequency of linkage of lights and storms when the storms involve summer lightning. There may reside another connection to geomagnetic forces.

As for pirates, lootings, burnings, and such, there is nothing in Kettle Point history that points toward such events as fact. But one never knows. What can one make out of sporadic, though persistent, claims of such crimes?

When I looked into the lore surrounding luminous things, both lights and the Light, there are always those who choose to find something ominous in such things even when the effects are benign or benevolent. It is said that spirits can call us to the Light and that the only issue of propriety is whether it is one's time for the call. There is the story symbolism of luminous spirits or beings. But what is that other than a reminder that we are the Creator's offsprings and have that luminosity within us as birthright?

My search has taken me into examination of ancient crafts where one finds talk of the Great Lights. In these quarters the view of the Light is truth and knowledge. To share knowledge is to bring light through the practice of time-honored rituals. The skittish among us demonize such sharing as the work of secret societies. But I now understand that there are not really any secrets about the Light, just things we have temporarily lost touch with. Information that is really encoded in our bodies and souls.

The first glimmer of this for me was on the lakeshore at Ipperwash Provincial Park. It was only the second time I had seen the lights and it was a night of singular beauty, the sky crackling with stars and the Milky Way a thick bejeweled belt from horizon to horizon. It was if the lights had a message for me that night, as one orb rapidly descended from space and another shot out of the lake. The moment filled me with a renewed knowing that everything there is came from the light of the moment of Creation and that everything yearns to return to it.

It was many years before I understood that we can glimpse through that origin point of Creation, look across time and space as it were. One old native elder near Watersmeet suggested as much to me during my Michigan visit. But I did not understand what he said until a year ago up at Pinery Provincial Park. I have a favorite there among some trees that has always been calming for me. There I saw light emerge from an animal den at the base of a tree. This is what the elder had told me, to look for an opening to unseen worlds. What I saw in a fleeting glimpse was a swirling like a pinwheel galaxy.

Some things you just know in your bones. Some things do not require scientific proof. I know I just did not see an optical illusion when I looked in that hole. No, my friend, I looked down the deep well of time and space. For a moment, however brief, I stood before a portal back to the Light. That is what I think we have around Kettle Point, portals for we mortals.

Black Shuck of Kincardine

C anine references in ghost lore are fairly common. This is certainly the case in Ontario. There the ghostly dogs of European origin seem to mingle and blend into the native references to wolf spirits. Even the echoes of American Indian tales of wolves are blends of various tribal mixtures involving Iroquois, Huron, and a variety of Algonquin voices.

Few of these dog and wolf stories have a direct connection to the Great Lakes, unless one counts the island tales common in Lake Huron's Georgian Bay and North Channel. Those variations have more to do with the haunting of the islands themselves, not the surrounding waters. While spirit dogs have haunted ships on the high seas, they are virtually unheard of on the large freshwater bodies. Prior to my foray into Canada the only such tales that came my way were obscure references from Lake Baikal in Siberia and Lake Titicaca in the Andes.

Milford hit me with a fully fleshed out story when I made my first fuel stop in Ontario. He was just trying to help me with directions to Oliphant when our conversation stumbled into yarns, ghost sightings and things weird. Even then he was the typical friendly Canadian; polite, modest, and mild of disposition. By the time I pulled out of Port Elgin I was as surprised at the story as at the Canadian gasoline prices.

*   *   *

There's a story or two or three up and down our piece of lake. If you look hard enough and if you find good people in a mood to talk, then you'll find a fair number of tales that will keep you up at night. I've heard my share between Sarnia and Tobermory. The one that stays with me is about Black Shuck.

Like any good story, it's not just bandied about for casual pass-ersby. It's the preserve of story connoisseurs who bring it out like they might a fine brandy or a good cigar. The occasions for such savorings might be periodic story repolishing among old friends or as a recognition gesture of story appreciation kinship. That's one of the most important things about a good story, like cognac, you don't want to waste it on the uncouth.

Now if you really want to hear all the details about Black Shuck you need to spend months round and about Kincardine. It would be best if you could point to a bloodline with some MacGregor and Owen in it. You can guess some of the ancestral angles on Black Shuck when you take measure of our place names like Dungannon and Douglas Point. Though away from Kincardine I am free to point out that in the old countries Black Shuck was shared by those of the Orange, those of the Green, those of the plaids, and those colorless men of the low shires.

In all fairness I must point out this spectral dog was once common in all British folklore. My professor nephew tells me that Black Shuck is out of the pedigree from the god Odin's war hound. The beast must have made an impressive landfall off a Viking ship, for terror of his arrival reverberated through Norfolk, Suffolk, Essex, and Devon until the day before yesterday. In the Highlands and on the islands Black Shuck must have pursued every last Celt into every crag and thicket.

The big dog left his print, as it were, all through the psyche of the island nation and then sent his offspring abroad with the island's seafarers to every continent. He does not inhabit ghost tales and folklore alone, he's also a staple in English literature. Tell me you haven't encountered an ominous dog or two in your readings. Some say that Sir Arthur Conan Doyle drew upon Black Shuck for his *Hound of the Baskervilles*.

What we have here is a direct lineal descendant of that old fellow, with a twist from Lake Huron. Our Old Shuck is a lakefarer and is seen on the water more than off. Not in the water mind you or shaking off a coat full of water. No, this mighty dog is known for a dignified stance in the prow of his boats. In a few cases he has even been mistaken for a ship's figurehead. That is until he moved and growled.

I've only had the privilege of seeing Black Shuck once. It was back when I was just a boy. He was standing in the front of a skiff that came ashore at Clark Point in a dense fog. Then he jumped onto the beach and ran inland. What's more he left no tracks. That's a common feature of Black Shuck encounters that end on the beach. There are never any tracks.

So no one ever knows where he goes when he goes inland. At least not exactly. The old version was that he was seeking out men to mark for death. Many of the old people thought that an encounter with Black Shuck meant that your days were numbered. That also was the way it was interpreted in the British Isles.

But I never met a man on the lake who felt that Black Shuck on a boat was an ill omen. There was more a feeling that he would even the score for lakemen who had been cheated by landsmen. Under this view he would show up on the doorstep of bankers, shippers, fish brokers, and such. Those so visited were destined for tribulations of biblical proportions. This meant everything from sores on intimate body parts to undignified deaths that provoke involuntary laughter among those who hear the accounts.

The evolution of this view of Black Shuck may have something to do with a failed social experiment in the United States. I'm talking about Prohibition. It seems that during that time Black Shuck served as a guardian spirit of sorts to smugglers and bootleggers. Now it so happened that Canadians of that day were a law abiding lot who nevertheless had deep reservations about U.S. policy on alcohol. It really seemed like supplying Canadian whiskey to our southern mates on this continent was the neighborly thing to do. Canadian authorities felt constrained to cooperate with U.S. authorities, but there was a noticeable lack of enforcement zeal in our area of lakefront.

So it happened that small boats made a brisk trade of liquor transport. It was said that a few boatmen took advantage of the legends and had in their employ large black watchdogs that would clamber about on the boats. Those dogs served the function of scaring off those whose casual curiosity might have otherwise prompted them to investigate darkened boats arriving late at night. They also served to reinforce the story of Black Shuck. Who knows, maybe they were from a litter sired by the giant canine.

Those liquor smuggling days are gone of course. Though I hear tell of boats bringing cigarettes and other black market items in from the U.S. Unfortunately I can't connect any ghost stories of dog spirits to this current activity.

The last Black Shuck story I heard had to do with fishing. As you know, there are those who occasionally get greedy in harvest of natural resources. The fisheries authorities can't be everywhere and investigate every catch. But it appears that Black Shuck fills the gap from time to time. At least if you find just the right fishing captain in Kincardine you will hear about a Toronto man who overfished and received dog teeth marks in his posterior as a reward.

Captain's Ghost of Tobermory

People and stories thin out a bit as you move up Bruce Peninsula way. There's a spareness to these environs and a feeling
that, while many have passed this way, none who have tar-
ried here have really owned it. There are stories on this stretch of
Lake Huron shore and, as spits of land often do, this parcel of Ontario
has its share of waterlogged lore. Still, the yarns and anecdotes
have a hard, rather than haunted, quality to them. Almost as if, in
some inhospitable way, ghosts might find the place too raw for them.

A circumnavigation of the upper Great Lakes soon convinces
the journeyer that this region has tales of rigorous weather in abundance and legends of hard-bitten lake types who spit in the eye of
cold, hunger, and dogged exertions in nearly every cove and estuary. I had heard many such accounts in my travels up to this point.
But the Bruce Peninsula told me without words. It was there in the
shoreline, the gnarled and tilted trees, and in the faces of those
whose outdoor trades kept them looking toward the northwest sky.

*Call him Jack, Jacques, or Jake — he goes by all three — and look for
him around warm stoves in Tobermory. He seldom ventures outside in
foul weather these days. He did his share of that in nearly four decades of
utility line work. He's but one generation removed from lake trades and
the narrative of stormy water still runs in his blood. One dare not call
him a haunted man, though he'll offer that he knew one such fellow quite
well.*

* * *

It was my Grandpapa Martin who first saw the Captain's Ghost
of Tobermory. He was not otherwise a frail man. No, he had done
just about everything there was to do on water from rafting logs to
pulling nets. He was the type of short, stocky, and tough man that
you get from the mix of French, Scots, Hurons, and Yank horse
thieves that dangle on our family tree.

The question is, did he also see the actual body of this ship's
master? He thought so when he was young, but his doubts grew
and his memories faded as he sank into dotage. Still he would talk

of that whippersnapper of a storm that came up in 1905 and cleaned
the lake of human presence. He remembered the immediate aftermath of the storm and recalled how groups searched the shore
around Wingfield Point. He recalled seeing the body bobbing along
the shore.

He ran to get help, being but in that unsure stage as a lad not
quite a young man. When the larger party returned the lake had
reclaimed its trophy and no body was in sight. Martin had a good
reputation, the adults believed him and launched more intensive
efforts. Boats were dispatched to MacGregor Channel. Soon debris
was found, including a battered pilothouse that was put under tow.

The wreckage was from the *Kaliyuga*, an antiquated wooden
steamer past its safe or useful life. One of those maritime artifacts
that shipping company greed kept afloat in spite of its space limitations and outmoded design. It was in rough service hauling iron
ore from Marquette to Erie, a trade for which it had physical and
economical limitations. Such a ship could not haul enough ton-
nage of such cargo to be competitive.

That noneconomical status figures in its fate, I would venture.
The story has it that the blasted vessel was steaming around se-
verely shorthanded, a shipping company move common when the
eye was on the bottom line. When such a rig is short five, six, or ten
hands, particularly in the rough labor department, then you have
men working twelve and fourteen hour watches. Such men cannot
fight a storm or even save their own lives.

Some also found irony and prophecy in the shipping company's
explanation that the ship's odd name derived from the Hindi words
for age of metal. Cruel joke on a wooden tub hauling rock. But I
have heard educated men say that the name comes down from ancient Sanskrit, in reference to a violent and vengeful god and a predicted age of strife.

Then, too, they labored under the circumstances of a new captain on his first vessel with master's papers. That is often a test of
crew and equipment in itself. No matter how many years as a first
mate, no matter how many voyages taking up slack for drunkards
and fools in the captain's quarters, it is different when a man takes
over a ship and he is new to the status. He has something to prove,
owners to serve notice on concerning his willingness to bring them
profit in weather fair or foul.

Such was the nature of Captain Tonkin, the first-season skipper
of the *Kaliyuga*. Apparently he was full of ego and was overconfi-

dent. What but pride and stubbornness would motivate a man to cast off with barely more than half of a crew? What else would take an experienced lakeman and send him nonchalantly into Huron in a foul season? What else would make him forget that Huron is a tricky water where nor'easters can turn and become nor'westers so that a man knows not where windward and leeward will be in the course of a blow? What else makes the experienced navigator throw training out the window and allows him to risk vessel, cargo, and crew on a chance run based on instinct?

That was the Captain Tonkin that Grandpapa Martin saw in ghostly form in the pilothouse of the wrecked *Kaliyuga*. That was the man whose body Grandpapa Martin most likely saw out on Wingfield Point. That was the man whose poor decisions took his entire crew with him.

Throughout a life on the lakes Grandpapa Martin thought and theorized about what brought Captain Tonkin to our peninsula. The impact on him was so great that Grandpapa Martin never completely got over trying to understand the chain of events that put that body on the shore in front of his eyes. He told me that it was likely a whole series of miscalculations, running one way on the lake and then the other, and not having the speed to find safe haven either way.

How well I remember the old man eyeing the tumbler of cognac and musing on such matters. There he was, forty or fifty years after the fact, trying to make sense of the tragedy, trying to assess blame. When the fire had burnt low he would eye the embers through the liquor and make pronouncements. He would start with low whispers that built up to vocal thunder. "He missed Main Channel," Grandpapa Martin would bellow toward the end of his rant. "He was headed into Georgian Bay, thinking he had Cove Island to his side, and instead came apart in shallow MacGregor."

Do not misunderstand me, I sympathize with Grandpapa Martin's feelings. I spent two years with the Canadian Army contingent in the Korean police action. I know what it is like to be witness to poor decisionmaking and the consequences of missteps. I appreciate how it leaves a man with doubts about the security and safety of earthly existence. But then again, I did not see a phantom nor a body appear and disappear.

Whenever a man finds himself exposed to danger and the elements while under the command of another man, he must ponder his fate and find empathy for others similarly situated. It makes no matter if he is a deck hand, a boiler tender, an artillery forward observer, or a utility lineman. In the worst of times he is apt to wonder if those who command are sane and competent. That is really what happened to Grandpapa Martin in his youth, the myth of the godlike and infallible ship's captain was broken for him just as his life on the lakes was getting underway. It was as if he had come to doubt God on the eve of his ordination as a priest and nevertheless gave lifelong service to a parish.

There is really only one convenient way into Tobermory from the south. That is the Highway 6 that brought you here. Seasonally you can get here from Highway 6's northern segment which originates up at Espanola and McKerrow and turns into a ferry transit in South Baymouth. Some visitors tell me that they drifted in or blew in. That is my cue to forgive them their figures of speech and let them know about one visitor who washed up. That is when I tell them about the Captain's Ghost of Tobermory.

Blackrobes of Georgian Bay

The stories of the Huron people are strangely absent along much of the shoreline of the great body of water named after them. Theirs is a sad tale of intertribal warfare, disease, European economic rivalries, and the worst aspects of victimization through missionary zeal. Some of the oldest legends place the Hurons' earliest settlements in that pleasant portion of Ontario between Lake Ontario and Lake Huron.

Perhaps more strange is the scarcity of tales about the experiences of the Huron on Georgian Bay, a body of water on which they were once a dominant force. Georgian Bay itself is the forgotten portion of Lake Huron, though it is almost as large as the lower two Great Lakes. In early times it was an inhospitable place. Even today the highways cannot hug the shoreline as in other portions of Lake Huron and the two other Big Sisters of Michigan and Superior.

It is this area from Lake Erie up to the Shores of Georgian Bay that was the scene of a holocaust for the Huron people. The time frame was the early Seventeenth Century. The means were varied, with guns and contaminated goods coming into play. Still, among those tutored in the old stories and ancient ways, there is an unshakable belief that the primary instrument of destruction of the Huron people was the Jesuit priests sent among them. This sentiment echoes down through generations of mixed blood survivors who still curse the depredations of the "Blackrobes."

Such anger-filled anecdotes are easy to find in eastern Canada. But it was not until I made a detour to Lake Nipissing that I was given a lead to an anti-clergy story with ghostly elements. Jacques' name was mentioned in a ceremonial sweat lodge on the shores of Lake Nipissing. An old one in the lodge said there was much to learn from the fate of the Blackrobes and advised me to seek out Jacques near Snug Harbor on the bay. The drive took me back to Canada Highway 69, up to Parry Sound, and, after several queries, out to an encampment near Killbear Provincial Park. Jacques was revved up and ready to go.

*   *   *

We saw one of the Blackrobes last night! They're still wandering, still looking for their Savior to give them the peace that they know they have not earned. How is it that men and their spirits can't figure out that any inner voice that commands cruelty to another is not the Creator's voice? Such voices come from twisted ghouls and Evil itself and are to be fought, not obeyed.

Good intentions and the blessings of bishops mean nothing in the face of the destruction of a people. There was nothing but arrogance in the view of "saving" a people with a culture thousands of years old. Save them from what? From the close relationship to the Earth that brought health and happiness for generations?

This story is in my blood. There were Huron men and women, mixed and almost pure, in my family on both sides. It's a story that has anger in it, but it's not about anger. It's a story with sadness in it, but it's not about sadness. It's about what all stories must be about: balance, imbalance, and restoration of balance. Almost every meaningful story is about the loss of purity and harmony, and then the long road back to it.

We've had almost four hundred years of the Blackrobes roaming the coastline, this stretch of Georgian Bay called the Thirty Thousand Islands. This is their purgatory, or hell, this piece of rocky water with its shoals, reefs, and barely submerged boulders. It's an area that shouts a warning to men with machines and refined manners. It says, stay back, the hand of the Creator is still fresh upon this place! Not that men of Western mind listened back then. Only a few listen now.

Did you know that in the 1630s the Huron numbered over twenty thousand? Did you know that the Huron were possessed of better lands and more influence than their Iroquois cousins? Few know those things, just as few know the sources of Huron-Iroquois enmity. Fewer know that the Huron had a form of peaceful civil governance that pre-dated the Iroquois Confederacy.

Then came the French with their trade goods that dazzled the people. The Huron took up trade with enthusiasm, in ways that weakened the voice of the elders. Those dazzled by cloth and jewelry were of a mind that the God of the French must be very powerful to provide them such gifts. It was that outlook that weighed in and won the argument to permit the Blackrobes to come live among the Huron.

Within a year, half of the Huron had perished, mostly from measles and whooping cough. The people were weakened, the able-bodied were dispersed for trade, and no one fished, hunted, or gardened for the elders or the babies. More sickness came, this time the smallpox that swept up the St. Lawrence and clear across the Great Lakes. The Blackrobes moved among the old villages of the Huron, touching the foreheads of the dying and claiming their spirits for their soul-hungry God. Again, half of the Huron were taken.

Admittedly, part of this tragedy was brought about by the weakness of the people. Some were seduced by the trade goods. Others were impressed by the God from across the sea. Perhaps some fell into drinking and other attractive vices at the hands of the French. So, yes, there is some measure of responsibility for not staying to the spirit path that gives protection. More of the Ojibwe did that and they came through better than the other lake tribes, but their remoteness may have helped them just as much.

In a matter of a handful of years the Huron became a decimated people, dispossessed of their large villages in fertile south Ontario and driven northward and westward. Still the Blackrobes pursued them with evangelistic zeal. The missionaries found their way even to these hidden bays and rocky inlets, preaching of a god that seemed more interested in death than life.

Eventually those Huron scarred by the changes and those who clung stubbornly to the old ways had enough of the alien God and came to wonder if their Creator had abandoned them because they had not resisted the French with sufficient vigor. With such thoughts circulating, it was natural enough that frustration and anger would be taken out on the Blackrobes. Perhaps the first such acts were simple acts of passion, a quick spear thrust by a man who had lost his children. Then after that you can expect more organized vengeance, with raids that burned mission settlements. Finally you come down to the capture of fleeing Blackrobes and skinning them alive. That's how the old stories go.

When I was young I was told such a thing happened here on Georgian Bay. I was told that those Blackrobes did not die manly deaths with clear minds and open hearts. Because of this, they could not go directly to their God from across the sea. Instead they still wander this shore and the nearby islands. That is why we still see them.

The old ones told me that only those with Huron blood see the Blackrobes. The blood quantum need not be large, but there must be some Huron in you. Those without Huron blood might hear the rusting of a passing Blackrobe or hear them reciting their pained prayers. Some outsiders have even heard the blood curdling screams of Blackrobes who were thrown to the fire. But so it goes among Europeans, they are plagued by hauntings because they did not die well.

It's not a story with a happy ending, at least not yet. The Huron remnants had their measure of revenge, then their wanderings continued. Many survivors were carried off by the Iroquois as captives. One small band fought with the French against the English in the French and Indian War. Some sought refuge among the Potawatomi. Another group kept to the old ways and became the Wendat or Wyandot.

Even those Wendat still make pilgrimages through this area to visit the places of their ancestors. Sometimes they come here to partake of the sweat lodge. There in the dark and steamy mist they see our ancestors. And they see the Blackrobes. It is natural that they take some measure of satisfaction in knowing that the spirits of our ancestors are at ease and those of the Blackrobes are not.

In some ways this story is like the old Ojibwe prophecy. The ancient Ojibwe foretold the arrival of the Europeans and said that it signified the end of the world. In a way it didn't, it signified the end of the native world of that time. Other peoples, including the Aztecs, had similar stories of phases in the world's evolution. Most also have views about the end of the current European world. Most feel that we will again return to the Earth-cycles and Earth-path of ancient times.

It is said when this change comes to Georgian Bay that we will be ready for it. Here on Georgian Bay we have not gotten so far away from the Earth-cycles and Earth-paths. It is also said that when the next end of the world comes, the end of the European world, then the Blackrobes are free to join their God from across the sea.

Lodge of the Lake

Story collectors often misinterpret initial references to tales about obscure subjects. This is all the more frequent when the subjects are shrouded in mystery and layered with multiple meanings. Was it in Sudbury or Espanola that I first heard the term "Lodge of the Lake?" Was it on Great La Cloche Island or on the dock in Blind River that I gained the initial hint that the Lodge in question was not a traveler's destination with hunting and fishing guides? Notes and memories are too jumbled to say at this writing.

It was on Manitoulin Island that I learned this lodge signified a group rather than a structure. In Wikwemikong I was told that it was an old fraternal order devoted to supernatural matters. In Kagawong it was suggested that such a lodge might still exist and meet on occasion.

There is no subject more fertile for folktales, conspiracy theories, and paranormal accounts than that of secret societies. The whiff of such things puts serious journalists and ghostbusters alike on the chase like hounds after the fox. It is an old obsession that afflicts high born and commoners, free thinkers and inquisitors. There is just something so tantalizing about the notion that small groups of secret operatives might control aspects of civil society, corporate structure, and religious denominations.

Few of the allegations about secret societies turn out to be true. It is often the case that such groups are simply fraternal orders with a desire for privacy. Occasionally such entities are total humbug calculated to agitate the yokels and to provide environments for cigar smoking and cognac sniffing in spouse-free environments.

So when I found Noel in his permanently parked motorhome near Sheshegwaning I was prepared to have all the allegations dissipate like dry ice vapor. He seemed as disorganized as one might expect of someone who lived knee-deep in Moosehead bottles. But as we sat on the rickety deck and watched the sun lay down a blazing patch across North Channel, he seemed concerned about shattering my illusions and unaware of how his story was more up my alley than he expected.

* * *

The concept of a lodge goes way back. Most directly from Middle English *loge*, but in turn out of Middle French and Old High German. The meaning started out as rough shelter, but gradually evolved into the temporary abode of itinerant workers, pilgrims, and building craftsmen. Later the term extended to those structures in which such groups would meet, share fellowship, and conduct business concerning mutual aid and relief of distress. Finally the term came to include the collective membership of those affiliated with benevolent orders. Thus one could speak of meeting in a lodge and belonging to a lodge. Such concepts were by the Middle Ages familiar to carpenters, soldiers for hire, seamen, brewers, scholars, magicians, and minstrels.

In modern times the meaning expanded to rustic inns and accommodations for servants. Then there's the zoological usage, a grouping of animals in a lair. And you have the translations from American Indian equivalents, signifying dwelling, ceremonial space, and groupings based on kinship or clan membership. So it's a loaded word.

Lodge of the Lake stretched the term even further. You could say it includes most of the attributes I've mentioned, plus some features of the supernatural. So it's not a lodge in the temporal or physical sense. No, it's a grouping of souls who possess the bond of having been taken from this mortal plane by the jealous reach of Lake Huron. Those on upper Huron, around Georgian Bay, along North Channel, and here on Manitoulin Island know bits and pieces about this lodge. It is glimpsed now and then by boatmen, fishermen, and woodsmen.

But few patterns emerge from these random encounters. The sightings cover almost two hundred kilometers of water and spits of land. The spirit presences in these gatherings vary and include a wide range of ghosts.

We can start with one that my grandfather and I saw many years ago down near Point au Baril. We were picking our way through fog, poling for rocks, when we heard the murmur of voices and saw an odd glow. We came upon a large open boat, like a whaler with fortified ends. In it were six men in a circle, heads bowed in prayer. One of the voices said, "Thank you, Brother McDougall." With that, grandfather started poling away and hushed me into silence.

When we gained the shore Grandfather told me that what we had seen was the lifeboat of the *Asia*, a wooden propeller-driven steamer lost back in 1882. The McDougall in question was the *Asia's* purser, John McDougall, one of six passengers and crew swept off the lifeboat in raging swells moments after the steamer sank. Seven others managed to hang on to the lifeboat, but all but two of those died of exposure and froze in the bottom of the boat. It was after this encounter that grandfather told me about the Lodge of the Lake.

"That's old McDougall," confided grandfather, "and he's leading those other five who were swept away with him in a session of the Lodge."

Grandfather explained that the Lodge of the Lake was an ad hoc affair that could meet anytime on any part of Lake Huron. But it seemed that it was seen mostly in our rough section, where most of the bigger ships had gone down. He also explained that the lodge could vary from three to nearly two dozen attendees with five or six being the most common number.

It turns out we have cousins who saw another meeting of the Lodge of the Lake. This one from the 1879 wreck of the sidewheeler *Waubuno*. The term waubuno is Algonquin and is said to refer to the dark arts or black magic. The ship itself went down over a hundred and twenty years ago near Parry Sound. But my cousins saw the wheelhouse of that sidewheeler floating just off Lonely Island. They saw an even dozen apparitions gathering around three lamps in the wheelhouse. Perhaps they were the crew members who crowed in there in the last moments before the ship broke up.

As for myself, I've seen these little meetings of lake victims twice since that day with my grandfather. Once it appeared as a canoe flotilla in Mississagi Channel, between Manitoulin Island and Cockburn Island. The canoes were in a ring, with prows pointed to the center. There were four canoes and they appeared to be lined up on the cardinal points of the compass. I heard rattles and drums and singing. Each canoe seemed to have two individuals with war paint. The mist drifted in and muffled them and obscured them from view. When the mist passed by there was nothing left but rippled water. Others have seen this grouping and identify the canoe occupants as long ago Iroquois scouts, separated from a large war flotilla and then lost in a storm. Such stories about lost Iroquois raiders are found in nearly every sound, strait, and passage on lakes Ontario, Erie, Huron, and Michigan.

My other sighting is a little harder to classify. It was certainly a weird sighting, a beat up commercial net boat in the middle of land-locked Kagawong Lake here on Manitoulin Island. It would take the mother of all storms to lift a fishing boat off Lake Huron and put it down in a big pond. The ghosts gathered on it were motley, too, an assortment of Indian guides, merchant seamen off freighters, a Yank charter boat captain blown across the lake, and a British Army officer in a red coat.

These odd assortments are more common than uniform groupings of ghostly victims. It is these diverse little bands that tend to include ghosts from more recent lake casualties. These are the meetings of the Lodge of the Lake that can pop up just about anywhere.

There are some who say that if you can see such things than you are destined for membership on this lodge of the afterlife. A claim like that is hard to substantiate with all the various forms that the Lodge of the Lake takes. But I can say that I saw my grandfather out on that battered fishing boat. He had been dead over twenty years at that time. I've never been much of a joiner, but I guess I'll find out if I've already been picked for membership.

St. Joseph's Kelpies

Stories were sparse as I headed up the northwest coast of Lake Huron toward her big sister Superior. This is not to say that there are none to be found, only that few leads came my way. As the reader probably detects by now, there is a certain randomness to my story collection method that relies partially on instinct and heavily on openness to what may come my way. This style, of course, invites the curious to explore on their own during their travels and discover things that eluded me.

The course followed toward completion of this book was one of steady pursuit of leads over nearly two decades. Even if the story was altogether different than expected, it was the lead, however fragmentary or deceptive, that usually brought me to the place where strange tales awaited the seeker. Such investigations were not filled with the recreational delights that marked many of my folktale ventures in Wisconsin. There is a big difference in the time compression that comes with a thousand mile drive and a five day limit than with repeated day trip sojourns close to home. The further I was from Eagletree Farm in Iowa County, Wisconsin, the more focused my enterprise and the less likely my personal dallying.

So I must chalk it up to sheer luck again that one totally whimsical side trip should produce a nice yarn from a new acquaintance. It did not come as a total surprise, the site into which I stumbled was a natural environment for such things. The impulse to detour out to St. Joseph Island on the way to Sault Ste. Marie was a last minute thing. Once on the island, the signs for Fort St. Joseph National Historic Park drew me like a magnet since such places have stories to tell whether or not there are people around to tell them.

No, the bigger surprise was in who had a story to tell, not that I heard one of the probably dozens that this spot likely could offer. It was a pleasant surprise to stop for a soft drink and meet Clara, a redheaded teenager whose eyes sparkled along with her stories.

* * *

Ghost stories? I've heard some, but they don't seem real to me. If by ghost stories you mean old dead guys running around throw-

ing a scare into people. I've never seen such a thing and all I have
to go on is what Uncle Bartlett told us when we were little so he
could scare us.

But strange things that we have on the island. Things I've heard
of and things I've seen, or at least think I've seen. We have a story
about a lake monster. We have a story of flying bright lights that
are probably secret U.S. aircraft. We have dozens of old Indian
legends. There's even an old French curse on one of the island families. But my favorite in all these things is about the kelpies. That's
because I think I've seen a kelpie at least once, maybe more.

I can tell that you have no idea what a kelpie is or how it works.
It's a magical being, a spirit creature the Indians would say and one
that they call a shapeshifter. You know, a thing than can appear in
more than one form. But those kelpies are not from Indian legends.
They are Scottish in origin and somehow they came here with Scots.
Maybe with some of my own ancestors? But they've been here a
long time and show no signs of leaving.

A kelpie in Scotland is a really evil spirit. There it usually appears as a horse or a shaggy man. It's always near the water and
comes out of the water over there. Or so says Uncle Bartlett. I've
heard it also appears as those shaggy Highland cattle in Scotland,
but I've never been further away than one trip to Toronto, so I can't
say.

But here on St. Joseph Island it can appear as just about anything. Uncle Bartlett says it often goes from man to bear or man to
wolf. When I thought I saw it the first time, it looked like it went
from a girl to a Shetland pony. The next time it went from girl to
terrier. There were other times when I thought I saw something,
but to tell you to truth I can't be sure what I saw. These things
move so fast!

Uncle Bartlett has some Indian friends who tell him we should
stay away from such things. He says they're more scared of a kelpie
than they are of their own evil spirits. That's because they believe
kelpies don't belong here and that there's no way to defend against
them. Uncle Bartlett says that they call them "bad medicine." I
guess that means their medicine men don't have charms to repel
them.

He also says that his Chippewa fishing friend believes that a
kelpie may have somehow crossed with a native wendigo, the local
spirit monsters. Apparently what they have in common is a hunger for human flesh. Uncle Bartlett likes to make me blush by refer-

ring to the mating habits of the wendigos and kelpies. But since he's an old bachelor, I get even when I tell him I probably know more about such things than he does. I just don't tell him that what I know is from books in school.

I'm not so sure about this thing of kelpies eating human flesh. That's the story from Scotland, where kelpies take people underwater and cut them up. Supposedly a kelpie eats everything but the liver and the liver floats to the surface. But I don't know anyone who's heard of such a thing on St. Joseph Island. I don't know that a liver would float, would it? I suppose there are lots of gooey and messy things that could float that someone might call a liver. After all, if a kelpie has already wolfed down some lungs, kidneys, and spleen, why stop at the liver?

There have been bodies in the lake that were cut up. Uncle Bartlett always says those are the work of kelpies. Dad says different. Dad says some were bodies banged up on the rocks, maybe even hit by big ship propellers. Most, he says, are the handiwork of U.S. criminals who haul their victims up here. He laughs at the idea of kelpies and explains what I've seen as the result of adolescent hormones. He thinks Uncle Bartlett got one too many bangs on the head in Korea.

I think Dad does not want to believe because the other part of the story is from Scotland. That says anyone who sees a kelpie is doomed to drown. Apparently nothing can protect you. Maybe this is why Mom doesn't even like me to cross a bridge. When I remind her that Uncle Bartlett and dozens of others have seen kelpies and not died she just says, "Not yet!"

Maybe it's just a little different here on St. Joseph Island. Maybe Lake Huron affects them differently than the North Sea over at Scotland. Since I've seen girls instead of shaggy men, it could be more like that thing I've read about that's in Germany. You know, that old story of the Lorelei. Young girls who sing songs to men on boats and pull them into dangerous places. That sort of thing wouldn't be necessarily fatal. It would only work on men who were lured by beautiful young things. Certainly not on another female. Besides, the girl I saw wasn't exactly model material.

If I wasn't for Uncle Bartlett and the others who have seen the kelpies I would think I was losing my mind. I'm too old for imaginary friends and too young for brain malfunction. So how do I explain what I've seen to myself? It doesn't matter so much what others think. I'm the one who has to live with what I've seen.

I've noticed that there are several ways that adults handle things like this. Some, like Dad, are very serious and quite rigid in not believing. Sometimes people like that seem so unhappy, especially when things happen that don't seem logical. Others, like Mom, are nervous about such things. Those people always seem so scared that something might happen that they forget to have a life. A few, like Uncle Bartlett, seem relaxed or, as he puts it, loosey-goosey. They're ready for anything and if one thing falls through they're ready for the next. Uncle Bartlett can be a bit of a flake, but I don't think I've seen the man have a bad day.

So as far as role models go, I think I'm leaning toward the relaxed type. It just seems that people who have a little magic in their lives have more fun. So what if it's only a kelpie?

Part IV
Soo to Twin Ports

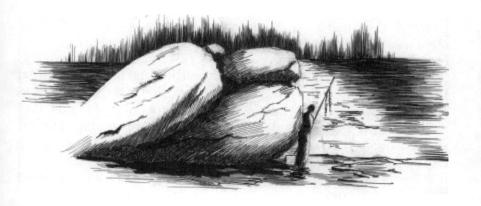

Boozhoo of Batchawana Bay

Huron's brooding gave way to Superior's exuberance as the traveler passed Sault Ste. Marie, Ontario. Once past the channel and interlocking transportation systems, there was a return to the familiar for me. Gitchi Gummi was an old friend upon which I have sailed, fished, and island hopped during three circle tours and many lesser forays to the likes of Thunder Bay, Grand Portage, the Upper Peninsula north shore, and Red Cliff Reservation.

Of all the Big Sisters, Lake Superior is the one that holds the most allure for me and is the one that figures immensely in my evolution as a collector of stories and a seeker of Earth wisdom. It is the lake of so many personal rites of passage: First traditional sweat lodge (followed by a dip in its icy waters), first sojourn on a commercial fishing boat, first descent into the dusty holds of grain ships, and first voyage on a rusty ore boat. No other area on Earth has so shaped my view of ecology, bringing me into a sense of Spirit of the Land, the vision of Eagle, and the power of Bear.

When I reach Superior I am no longer rooting around for leads nor dependent upon the mercies of strangers. Instead there's the embrace of networks, friends of friends, and families and clans that have "adopted" me. Thus many of these stories set on Lake Superior are in the context of breaking bread with longtime acquaintances, sleeping on the sofas of allies in environmental struggles, and sharing twelve-packs of beer under the Lake Superior moon.

The stop at Ronnie's craft and gift shop on Canada 17 was a natural. I had stopped twice before and had frequently seen him on the pow-wow circuit in northern Wisconsin and Minnesota. He has the natural Anishinabe[1] gift for storytelling and is possessed of the personal power to let those of European descent know that when they enter his shop they are in Indian Country. A casual conversation with him about Batchawana Bay produced this little story, which is perhaps about trickster spirits or perhaps about Anishinabe storytellers.

*   *   *

This is a local story. It's not a part of the Anishinabe tradition, but it takes off from some of it. The traditional stories are part of a system of spiritual beliefs and values. Stories such as this one might incorporate some of those values, but their point is more to take the occurrences of everyday life, explain them, and have some fun while you're at it.

There's always something beyond a story, no matter whether it's a conventional ghost story, an ethnic tall tale, or a strange whacked-out narrative about inexplicable events. Many stories have all these aspects to them and leave us flustered about what the hell is going on. That's the trick isn't it, finding the story behind the story? Isn't it strange how sometimes a story that is 99 percent fabrication can ring with an essential truth that touches our spirit? And isn't it frustrating how a story that is 100 percent authentic and verifiable can leave us in disbelief?

It comes down to whether the message reaches some part of us. A good story gives the listener a moment of *knowing*. But even then you must consider the various ways people hear and learn. If a story is beyond their capabilities — too horrible or too depressing — they will resist the moment of knowing.

But today we speak of lighter things. I want to tell you of the Boozhoo of Batchawana Bay. This is a trickster spirit much like the character of Wenebojo of the Ojibwe and Menominee down in Wisconsin. But it's not just an Anishinabe story here. This trickster afflicts and delights Indians and European Canadians around the bay. It's not a story from long ago, it's an ongoing force that shapes local events.

Nobody has actually seen this Boozhoo, but his presence is felt. Those with good powers of observation notice when he has passed their way. They know his touch upon events and objects. In fact, I use the term "Boozhoo tracker" for those I feel are practically sensitive to their surroundings. A good Boozhoo tracker knows the seasonal patterns of this mischievous spirit, they know how it dovetails with the Anishinabe calendar of the cycle of moons and how it is part of the worldwide native system of the Medicine Wheel. A good tracker can see Boozhoo's breath in shaking aspen leaves and see his tracks on rippled bay ice.

Our Boozhoo must be a descendant of the original Boozhoo brothers. Those were the sons of Winonah and the Spirit of the West. Those brothers are enshrined in the sacred stories of the Anishinabe, but they are also the subject of profane and laughable stories. It is a good thing when a people understand the short distance between the sacred and the profane.

The oldest of these brothers was Maudy-Boozhoo. He was the serious one. He was very manly, but a little full of himself. So much so that he often became the butt of jokes, particularly those originating with his younger brothers. That is his connection to humor, the stuffed-shirt who can't laugh at himself and doesn't know when he's laughable.

Puka-Boozhoo was the second son and was beloved by the people. He disappointed his father and older brother by not pursuing serious endeavors. He was not one for spirit quests or trials of strength. He was the one who brought laughter to the Anishinabe. He did so with the vehicles of dance, song, and storytelling. He knew the strong medicine of laughter and practiced it as a good magician.

The third son was Cheeby-Boozhoo and he was the brother most devoted to the spirit path. But he understood better than his oldest brother that spirit brings Light, not heaviness. He was an example to the people to open their hearts even in struggle and to laugh in the face of danger. He was the author of chants and maker of music that lighten the footsteps and quicken the blood of the Anishinabe.

Nanay-Boozhoo was the youngest brother. It is he who traveled to Wisconsin and became Wenebojo. But he is known by other names in other places. Some say that he was known among the southern cousins of the Anishinabe, the Potawatomi, the Ottawa, the Sac, the Fox, and the Kickapoo. He was the one who taught the most lessons to the people, He possessed every human flaw and virtually none of the character one would expect of Anishinabe. His was a life of mishaps, errors, and blunders. He was an enduring example of what not to do. His stories produced laughter and tears, especially among those who recognized some of his weaknesses in themselves.

If I had to pick the family line of our Boozhoo I'd say he's a direct descendant of Nanay-Boozhoo. So maybe it's just like it's been with the Anishinabe for hundreds of years, cousins drifting back and forth across the lake between Ontario and Wisconsin. So who knows, maybe a grandson or great-grandson of that Wenebojo came back here to visit the places of the great Anishinabe emigration and liked Batchawana Bay enough to stay.

No one knows the time frame of his journey or when he made the transition from spirit-man to plain spirit. Both the stories have been here for a long time. Probably since before the arrival of the

Europeans. But soon they were mixed up in it just like they are in everything else around Lake Superior. Interference and intercourse makes it hard to draw lines about who influenced what at this point.

Our Boozhoo of Batchawana Bay shows some of this confusion. There's some preoccupation with gadgets and material things, things that are not major Anishinabe interests. Now, admittedly, this interest often comes out as a tendency to gum up these machines. So if the distributor wires on your truck are crossed up, you'll know Boozhoo was around.

It's amazing how much of Boozhoo's influence is felt in the automotive world. Practically everyone I know around here has experienced his destructive tinkering with their vehicles. This is the explanation for diesel fuel in the gas truck and vice versa. This reason why parking brakes somehow get released and allow cars and trucks to coast merrily into the lake. It's true that many of the vehicles are what's known in Indian Country as "rez cars,"[2] our equivalent of the ghetto cruiser. But I've seen brand new SUVs fall prey to Boozhoo tampering.

Boats are also inviting objects for our Boozhoo. If the outboard clunks out on you miles from home after you just had it serviced, well, you know who was tampering with it. Same thing if your new shiny hull has a leak that just doesn't make sense. And if your boat is sitting on lake bottom while tied to the dock, the culprit is as obvious as the nose on your face. You've been Boozhooed.

In this sense the spirit of Boozhoo must have the attitude of the Plains Indians with their "counting coup." It's as if there's a point system to all this. There was the old Anishinabe custom of bear-slapping, a daring game of hitting black bears on the rump. But nothing as repetitive and frequent as getting Boozhooed is for some people. Some people I know have been Boozhooed on their truck, their boat, their ATV, their hot water heater, and their stereo all in the same week. A few I know have even been Boozhooed with their birth control devices.

I know this makes our Boozhoo seem alternately like a juvenile delinquent Bart Simpson or a dunderhead Homer Simpson. Maybe he is in a way. But for those of us around Batchawana Bay the issue isn't what Boozhoo does to us. It all comes down to how we respond to those challenges and setbacks. That's the spirit of teaching all the way back to Boozhoo's ancestor Nanay-Boozhoo.

Grain Ship Ghosts

The drive up Canada 17 to Wawa is one of my favorite sketches of Lake Superior shoreline. One reason for this sentiment is the uncluttered nature of this highway and the views it affords. The section between Pancake Bay and Michipicoten Harbor is a scenic byway and transverses the heart of Lake Superior Provincial Park. After Wawa, Canada 17 veers into the interior and does not again skirt Lake Superior until Marathon on the Pic River.

Michipicoten Harbor is the best spot for lake lore on the east end of Superior. Old-timers are quite capable of recounting the history of the big fur companies, the yarns of the voyageurs, and the superstitions of boatmen and woodsmen. There are probably a good baker's dozen ghost stories associated with the Michipicoten River. Not to mention tales of spooky events out on Michipicoten Island.

So it was a bit of a surprise that the best ghost story to come my way on my last Michipicoten Harbor trip had a link to the grain trade from the west end of the lake. Perhaps it is not so strange, given that Michipicoten Harbor produces sons who ply the lakes in vessels of every sort. Ernest is one of those sons. Though now retired, he gave nearly forty years to the lake and still has a son and grandsons engaged in maritime trades. He finds mystery in the transit of grain from the western prairies across the Great Lakes and on to the ports of the world. He believes it's a trade that tempts fate and generates ghosts.

* * *

Those grain vessels are ripe for tragedy. From the very beginning of the grain trade they were the ships that pushed the November limits. If there was wheat in the grain silos of old Port Authur up on Thunder Bay then they would keep hauling it until the lake was downright dangerous. They constantly tempted fate in November and sometimes into December. If they were lucky they would just get frozen in on the upper lake at the grain dock. If they weren't lucky they'd join the ships claimed by Lake Superior.

That's why even today the rigs hauling grain have ghostly visitors. Grain sailors are a superstitious lot and often consider such visits as bad omens. But I never found that to be true. I saw a phantom on nearly every grain run I sailed on. They always looked more lost than spooky.

Even today those hauling grain see out of place apparitions. Sometimes in the passageways and sometimes in the galley. My son saw one on a steel catwalk topside and the darn thing stepped aside to let him pass. This was in foul weather in seas where footing and handholds were matters of life and death.

This all has a local connection because these crew ghost sightings were most common out in the main shipping lanes south of Caribou Island. There are reasons for this that we will get to. But this was the area where lake sailors were always alert for strange sights. It's a tradition that is nearly one hundred years old and it's linked to another ghost sighting we'll talk about.

I guess it all goes back to November of 1902. That's when the *Bannockburn,* a sturdy grain ship in the trade for over a decade, decided to risk a late season run down lake from Port Arthur. It was a questionable decision then and was argued with vigor for decades after she pulled away from the dock. Quite a few of the older wooden boats learned that you could not cheat November storms. When the steel hulls came along some thought they were invincible. The *Bannockburn* was a steamer built in England in the late 1800s. She was in a line of steel ships produced precisely for the Great Lakes trade. As you know, major ocean-going vessels could not ascend the lakes until the St. Lawrence Seaway. But in those days steel vessels could indeed be sent uplake if they fit the tight dimensions of the St. Lawrence Locks and the Welland Canal. These design limitations in turn make for some odd usage patterns. You had steamers like the *Bannockburn* built with holds for cargo, but powered like they were tugs. Often, in good weather at least, they would tow grain barges.

But she wasn't towing anything in November of 1902. She shoulda never left the dock. But money being the human motivator that it is and shipmaster pride also figuring into such things, the *Bannockburn* went out on its late season jaunt and was seen making headway gamely, if not easily, halfway down the lake. She was even noted in the logs of other ships out on the lake at the time. But those who saw her also noted the heavy twenty foot seas at the time they passed her.

Well, the seas likely grew, probably to thirty foot, maybe to forty foot by the time she was off Caribou Island. After that everything is pure speculation. The main theory is that she made a run for the protection of Michipicoten Island and broke up on the shoals of Caribou Island. The dangers of this approach were well known to lake mariners. But that foul night was marked by a bad turn of human conduct. You see, Canada did not like encouraging these late November runs, so the authorities shut down the Caribou Island lighthouse as a way of closing the navigation season. But is doesn't appear that adequate notice of the closure was given.

So if the *Bannockburn's* master was looking for the light it was in vain. He was taking his vessel into one of the most treacherous stretches of water on the lakes and the worst hazard on the main shipping lane. Caribou Island has very dangerous shoals that extend considerably out from the island. It's said that if you can see Caribou Island in foul weather, well, then you're already sunk and just don't know it yet. These hidden rocks extend several kilometers out from shore. You could see where they're particularly dangerous in heavy seas. Calm lake and fog and it means you've run up on the rocks and simply have the embarrassment of calling for the tugs. Forty foot seas and you got bigger problems. Problems like a trough slamming you on the rocks and breaking a steel keel like a matchstick.

That's probably how she disappeared. No one knows for sure as there were no survivors and the only wreckage was a lifeboat oar and a life preserver that washed up on the U.S. side months later. Odds are that the whole crew went to the bottom in her.

The real interesting part is that other ships and shore observers continued to report on her for the next few weeks. One telegram would say she was run aground on Michipicoten Island, another that she was awaiting repairs up on an isolated bay, and others still that she was now underway and headed home. All these reports were either wishful thinking or sightings of a ghostly phenomenon.

Such things like that have happened for years among mariners. Lost ships are seen by those on watch in the waters where they were lost. Sometimes they are crewless and decrepit. Other times they look brand new and are bustling with their full complements. No one who has long sailed says anything ill of a mate who reports such a sighting. It is just chalked up to the unknown forces at work in deep water.

As time went on the *Bannockburn* itself was not seen so much anymore. Though I saw it myself one stormy November. It's still seen sometimes in the area between Michipicoten and Caribou islands. But that's a rare thing these days, at least compared to the ongoing sightings of the haggard crewman. Yes, it's usually just one, though I've heard of others from time to time.

There's always been speculation about who this grain boat ghost is. The lost crew left kin around the lake so there's many descendants to claim. Some think it's the *Bannockburn's* master, Captain Wood. That doesn't wash with me, unless you're talking about sightings of multiple ghosts with someone with the bearing of a master among them.

No, my theory comes down to Artie Callaghan. He was the 16-year-old wheelsman who went down with the *Bannockburn*. He fits the youthful and poor dressed figure that is seen on today's grain ships. Artie has the biggest reason not to rest in peace for these many years. Despite his age, he was sole support for a brood of siblings in a troubled family. Like most from his ship's crew he was from Kingston. I sailed with fellows from Kingston and was told by the family men among them that you don't go home to Kingston unless you've made the pay list and have cash to bring home with you.

So maybe that's all this is, waiting on wages from the grain trade. If so, this is a matter for an accountant, not an exorcist.

Pukaskwa Weendigo

lmost twenty years before my stop in Michipicoten Harbor I made my first drive around Lake Superior. At that stage I was not chasing stories, supernatural or otherwise. Instead it was an unusual prod that sent me around the shores of Gitchi Gummi. That first journey flowed from a bit of grandfatherly advice from an elder at Red Cliff.

The occasion was my first sweat lodge, which was undertaken more out of cultural curiosity than spiritual calling. A friend and fellow Vietnam veteran brought me into that space because he sensed something unsettled in me, some sense of incompleteness. So we sat in the hot dark confines with others seeking renewal or direction. At one point more glowing red stones were brought into the lodge and an old man pointed a bony finger at me and said, "Find your connection to the Earth, make a journey around Lake Superior, go to the Pukaskwa country, and face your fears."

His directive sent a chill through me that I wanted to shake off. But my friend advised me to find out what was waiting for me on the north side of the lake. He respected the old fellow as a seer and wiseman. So he prepared me ceremonially, psychologically, and logistically. I was to find a monster who was waiting for me up on the White River in Ontario.

They sent me up past Thunder Bay to that stretch of Canada 17 that hugs the north shore of the lake. In the Marathon vicinity I was to look for Highway 627 and veer southeast into the wilds. The directions sent me to Heron Bay and steered me to a guide who went by the name of Bear. He was an extremely large Anishinabe man. He was to take me down the trail into the Pukaskwa National Park and then deep into the forests.

He did that and much more. He taught me as much as anyone else ever had. He brought me to the place where I saw the things predicted in the sweat lodge back at Red Cliff. However, what I found there was the intimate type of story meant only for my heart and soul. But on the hike in Bear told me many stories. This is the last one he told me before he left me to the silence of my solo retreat.

* * *

A man alone who is fasting can see many things, some real and some in his imagination. Fasting breaks down barriers so you can see into the spirit world and see the signs that spirits send your way. So it is a good tool when used in a good way.

But the other side of hunger is not of much help. No, starvation is almost the opposite of the fast. It is not controlled, it is not the peaceful way of the spirit path. It is desperate and it gives a man strange thoughts and bad impulses. It is important to recognize the difference in the signs seen in the fast and the delusions of starvation.

I tell you this because I have seen the Weendigo. It's one of those things that you're better off not knowing about, better off never seeing. You're never the same after an encounter like that. You not only experience horror, you reorganize your thinking and your insides. You pass through a barrier that others don't understand and when you come out on the other side you're a different person.

The story of the Weendigo was told often when I was a boy. It was told to scare us, like old men like to do at times. But others said the Weendigo was a thing of the past, something that died when old ways and hard living were left behind. A few others said no, the old things may be hard to find, still they are out there for those who look.

Pukaskwa's Weendigo is a survivor of a vast race of Wendigook, the Cannibal giants that the Anishinabe found as they pushed further north on their great migration. The Wendigook were known for their craving of flesh and the terror they struck into the people's hearts in the north country. Not only were they vicious, they were never satisfied. As they eat, they grow and they crave more, and eat more and so forth. So they are always starving. It is always that way with cravings.

Their smell gives them away before you can see them, since they most often approach in blinding storms. They are the color of death, the greenish-gray of a corpse. Their skin is like cracked leather, only leaking out pus and clotted blood. Except when viciously chomping on humans, their mouths are locked in a perpetual silent scream. Their eyes are sunken, but have a look that can kill the weak.

When I was still a boy our clan's medicine keeper told me that I would be a hunter and tracker. He told me that he had a dream that I would track the Weendigo and surprise it. This, he said, would be my mark as a hunter and tracker. More importantly, it would put the Pukaskwa Weendigo on notice that Anishinabe had learned through the generations how to survive even the greatest horrors. It would know that we were able to find it in its den during its dormant time in the warm months. So it would be cautious about angering us.

Learning to track the Weendigo is much the same as learning the lessons of hunting anything. You learn its habits. You listen to the stories about how it came to be, what its place in the world is, and what lesson its spirit has to teach. Then, you do what any true hunter must do, you dream of your quarry, you meet it first in a vision, and you ask the Great Spirit and the sacred directions to send it to you. This is how you learn the medicine of the hunt.

So, yes, I was eventually able to track and surprise the Weendigo. But I think I was more surprised at that moment than it was. It was if it had felt me coming for a long time and was resigned to the inevitability of the encounter. The surprise was what I felt in myself, the recognition of a tie or a bond to this horrible thing. That is what hunting medicine can do for you. It gets you ready for lessons and moments when you feel at one with everything. There's strength in a moment like that. That's what prevents life from being sucked out of you even in an encounter with a horrible thing.

The Pukaskwa Weendigo comes on the driving storms out of the North. The ones so bitter and so cold that wind feels like the caress of a porcupine and that the sap in the trees explodes. This is when I went tracking the Weendigo. I had planned well, so I thought. I had food and warm clothing. But the tracking of the Weendigo exhausted the provisions and went beyond the limits of equipment. In the end it was necessary to learn that I only had myself when it comes to confronting fearful things. I had to learn that you must exhaust the external resources before you can really test the internal ones. When my journey of cold and hunger took me to that point then I could see the Weendigo and know in that moment that I possessed greater medicine power than it did. In that moment it felt as if my look could shrink it. That was the moment of victory here in Pukaskwa.

It is from such encounters that you really learn about yourself and about what you're made of. You learn to understand the difference between those things which operate on the physical level with us, those things which are in the inner level of self, and those things in the story realm which hold the knowledge about our people. The Weendigo works on all those levels. My encounter really helped me understand the story realm.

I now understand that the Anishinabe suffered deeply in the harsh winters of long ago. There are lessons about thinking ahead here. There are lessons about harmony with the seasons and the creatures who feed us. There is much to learn here about deprivation, suffering, excess, gluttony, addiction, and lack of self-control. So in the handed down lessons there is not only teaching about horror and facing fear, but about planning, foresight, and restraint. Perhaps it's no coincidence that the word weendigo is closely related to older Anishinabe words meaning to "take care of oneself."

What is also interesting in the old stories about Wendigook is how they come into being. It is surprising how many ways it can happen. It often happened to someone who chose to engage in improper sorcery and did it to themselves. Just as often it was the result of a curse on another. It even happened that an effigy could be made and enchanted into being a Weendigo. Then somewhere along the difficult wanderings of the great migration you have Wendigook become a race or species. In this shift from isolated individual monsters to a group of raiders you might just find the remnant memory of group ritual cannibalism encountered along the way.

Then, too, you wonder if the old stories didn't anticipate the monsters we will fight in the future. Not only the machines that literally eat the land, but the distant lurking presences that seek to eradicate different ways of living. By this I mean the things that crave control in the farthest reaches of the earth and over the earth itself. They can be mining companies headquartered in London or banks in Zurich. But maybe they are insatiable Wendigook too?

There are many things to be feared and then conquered. Some in those deep woods. Some inside ourselves. And even a few lurking in distant dens where the skills of the tracker, the hunter, and the possession of hunting medicine are needed to find and confront evil. Ho, there is something stirring ahead! Maybe this is the place where you will meet what is waiting for you?

Marie of the Lakes

Women have been elbowed aside in much of the lore of the Upper Great Lakes. This is true of folktales, ghost stories, and the exuberant category known as whoppers. In the transition from peaceful tribal agrarians to conquest of new territories in the age of global expansion, most of the tone and rhythm of stories told by women was lost. So many of the Great Lakes stories are about robust outdoor pursuits in timeframes that preclude much participation by women.

Story collectors will also tell you that women often tell stories differently and in different settings than men. Odds are that you won't hear a story told by a woman at a boatlanding or in a tavern. But the odds of hearing such a story improve if you have the ear to pick up what is said in a farmhouse kitchen or in the serving line of a church supper. One of my earliest female sources down in Iowa County, Wisconsin, told me that a man would tell a tale about the accumulated manpower, draft horses, and equipment required to tackle the threshing of grain on large acreage. But she also offered that the woman on that same homestead could tell you exactly how many chickens were roasted, how many pies were baked, and how many gallons of sumac lemonade were consumed by the threshing crews.

The reader will note that most of the narrators in this collection of stories are men. This is not by design. It probably has more to do with who I am and who is willing to talk to me. It's not that easy to gain access to those kitchen conversations, be they farmhouse or fishing cottage. The task is all the more difficult when you're a large burly type of inscrutable countenance.

Yvonne had no such reservations since she was in a public space and expected to regale visitors with period conversation at the Old Fort William open-air museum near Thunder Bay. It was one of my favorite stops on my 1991 Lake Superior circle tour and Yvonne was one of the many excellent young historic reenactors that I met at this fine facility. The following, offered up after conclusion of her practiced remarks, proved she had also been listening to the storytellers who had passed this way.

*   *   *

You would be surprised how often visitors tell me stories of long ago. Some are just little historical curiosities, things so parochial that one would not be interested unless you lived in the setting of the story or were family to its principals. But there are times when jolly old men will flirt with me, wink their crinkled eyes, pull their trousers up as if to hide their bellies, and then tell me a story of strange and spooky things. Often their wives will roll their eyes and walk away. Not because the story is unbelievable, but because of the delight their husbands take in telling the stories to someone my age.

One such story I have been hearing with increasing frequency is about Marie of the Lakes. I was already familiar with the story from childhood in Thunder Bay, my Grandpapa Ross loved to tell it. But I did not know how much credibility to attach to it and I only know Grandpapa Ross's version of it. I would discover here that there was much more to this story than we here locally knew.

Perhaps the strangest thing about all this is that I started to see a presence here that I think must be Marie of the Lakes. You may think I have an overactive imagination or that I have spent too much time dressed up in clothes from the 1700s. But to tell you the truth, at first I thought some of the others who work here were pulling a little trick on me. I no longer think that. My encounters with Marie are outside rules that apply to the human body. Things like floating along slightly above ground and seeing only her face in a water pail.

Marie was one of the first women to live a European life of sorts on the western Great Lakes. This was so even though she was mixed blood herself, probably of Micmac and French. Some of the stories have her Ottawa and English or Huron and Scottish. But the French and Micmac claim makes the most sense, since it agreed she came out this way from eastern Canada and had been taken as a child to Paris.

It sounds like she had an adventurous life back in those times. She was once captured by pirates on an ocean voyage. She survived a shipwreck another time and was picked up by whalers. Twice a widow, she finally wed a man in the fur business and traded a life on the seas for a life in lake country. That is how she came to our area after the British assumed the lead role in Canada.

Marie became well-known for her efforts to help other widows and their children in those fur outposts. She became a saint-like figure in many of these places. There is some suggestion that she was something of a healer, although it was common for women in her role to nurse sick traders and dispense medicines. The legends suggest she could heal by touch, too. Had she been of pure European blood and in better standing with the Catholic Church she might have been canonized. As it is the memory of her only hangs on in pockets here and there.

Another feature of this story is the allegation that Marie acquired healing power through an unusual circumstance. One of her trips on the Great Lakes brought her in between warring tribal bands and she became a captive of an Iroquois chief who himself had extraordinary gifts of magic. When Marie's honesty helped him identify a wrongdoer the chief gave her the gift of the healing arts.

It was after her death that the claims of these powers took on a larger aspect. After she was seen as a ghost there was soon a belief that she was still a healer. Added to the mix was the belief that she was now a guardian spirit. People thought that she showed up wherever there was sickness or misfortune. Oddly enough, the epidemics that had recurrently swept through the Great Lakes outposts lessened after these appearances.

This guardian spirit aspect also had a gender angle. She became strongly associated with protecting women, particularly women braving the rigors of Lake Superior. There were circumstances where a lone woman on a storm-tossed boat survived when burly men did not. These survival incidents were attributed to Marie's protective presence. In some cases she seemed to pick out young women, almost as proteges, and guard them throughout their lives. One has to wonder if the guarding went beyond into guiding. Some of these women favored by Marie lived long lives, despite many rigors and hazards. One grand old lady from Red Rock told me that she suspected that Marie of the Lakes came to dwell within these young women, but she made no differentiation between reincarnation and possession, so that theory was a bit jumbled.

Older gentlemen travelers who tell me about such things say that Marie of the Lakes was known over a wide territory. At least they have mentioned places as far flung as Mackinac, Green Bay, and Victoria Harbor. Beyond that, there seems to be a connection to all the old military forts and trading stations. The most suggestive of these are the tales linking her to Fort William.

It makes one wonder if she is somehow lulled into haunting this place because of what has been recreated here? Between the feel of the physical setting and the reenactments of those of us who work here, it just might seem like a fitting place for a spirit such as her to use as home port. Maybe there is something about what happens at places like this that trigger the reactivation of spirits, pull them back among us.

When I have talked about such things with others here they mock me mildly about being Marie of the Lakes myself. One young man suggests he is willing to perform an exorcism on me, but I think he has something else in mind. One older gentleman who often visits here also jokes about me being Marie of the Lakes. He tells me, with a wink, that I am heir to a treasure of gold buried by one of Marie's trader husbands.

I am not sure if I believe in past lives or possession. I am not sure that I believe that the spirit of a dead person can live in us and shape us. But I am open to the possibility that a kindred spirit from the past can reach out and touch a current life. That is what I believe happened between myself and Marie of the Lakes.

Haunted Isle Royale

Wisconsin folklorist John Gard claimed that his home state
had the highest density of ghost stories to be found any
where. Twenty years of collecting stories in the Midwest
has confirmed the reasonable basis of this assertion in my mind,
especially viewed on a statewide basis involving many square miles
and varied local cultures. These same travels, however, also brought
me to the occasional locality that was even more blessed propor-
tionately with tales of odd happenings and lingering spirit presences within its small confines.

The southwest journey along Lake Superior's north shore is not
immediately suggestive of such possibilities. There is a certain in-
definiteness to this stretch of coast that comes with sudden transition in national identity. This is the only shoreline on the Great
Lakes shared by the United States and Canada. Further, there is
the sense that the borders were set as much through the ignorance
of distant officials as through geopolitical design. It is said that
those who negotiated the Jay Treaty of 1794 did not know the location of the Pigeon River relative to other features when they se-
lected the river as the new border. The main portage to the interior
lies to the south and the angular border line charted northeast across
Lake Superior also put an island jewel in U.S. waters.

*These quirks played out in many ways that displaced trading compa-
nies, altered hunting and fishing patterns and provided an unusual settlement evolution to the place called Isle Royale. The island itself is only a
few miles from Minnesota and Ontario, but is part of Michigan and can
be reached by ferry from the Upper Peninsula. I knew nothing of that at
the time I rode the other ferry from Grand Portage on the mainland to
Windigo on Isle Royale. On the trip over I met Leo, who grew up on the
island, and who was only too glad to share the secrets of his birthplace.*

* * *

My dreams still take me back to Isle Royale almost every night.
Even though I've long lived with my daughter down in Two Harbors I still think of Isle Royale as home. It's where I was born in a

summer nearly eighty years ago and where I lived until I went into the Navy.

It's a haunted place, you know? Full of ghosts! Full of strange sounds, strange sights, and strange sensations. At one time it was full of strangely wonderful people. Now it's just a summertime destination, a place for city people to visit so that they can get a feel for what it was like up here when lives were lived here.

It's those lives that were lived here that still vibrate in this place. That's what the hauntings are. That's what I still see on the island. No sir, I'm not the only one. There's hardly a one who was reared out here who doesn't sense what I'm talking about. It's just that some of us can see it or hear it better than others.

People have always come and gone from Isle Royale. Often people lived here seasonally, even after the Ice Age when the first men with spears discovered there were caribou to be hunted out here. That was probably close to five thousand years ago. The caribou didn't disappear from the island until my childhood. But I have seen the ghosts of caribou and so have others.

The island was a hunting and fishing paradise for almost all of that five thousand years. A handful would stay over in the winters, sugaring until the waters cleared in spring. Then in summer more people would come out to hunt and gather berries. It wasn't for nothing that the Ojibwe called the place Minong, which means "a good place to be." Those native ghosts are here, too, from all the way back to those ancients who wandered the newly carved lakes and way up to the mixed bloods with the first outboard motors. I've seen the ancients in hide boats in Siskiwit Bay and I've seen the ghost of the half-Finn, half-Ojibwe guide who had a hut near Cumberland Point.

The island was always in transition. There was always someone coming and going right from the beginning, always some survival issue or economics or politics pushing on people. That's the stuff that stirs ghosts, you know. Some say that the Sioux, French, British, and later Americans squabbled over it and opened it to immigrants from far away places. In the end it was as much Scandinavian as anything else. That's my blood and the blood of the last group of fishermen out here. Those ghosts are here, too, and I know more than one old Norwegian son of Isle Royale who heard the call of fishermen in the mist, long after the last commercial boats pulled out of island harbors.

I think there's always been a strong sense that the island was a thing on its own, that it didn't really belong to any nation. Of course that National Park Service thinks different these days. Isle Royale was legally in Michigan, but hardly anyone paid any attention to that. There wasn't much Michigan presence out here and most who needed to do mainland business did it in Minnesota. Even a little bit of bootlegging went on with Canada. Those packets and night runs still haunt the west channel too.

Despite the tug-of-war between the U.S. and England, those who lived on the island did as they pleased while alive and continue that obstinacy in the afterlife. It's a long Isle Royale tradition. Didn't matter if the British-run North West Company had to pull back and leave the island to the American Fur Company, the Ojibwe stayed loyal to North West and simply went to Canada to do business. Our family heard from the older white settlers on the island that Ojibwe ghosts made a long custom of canoeing from Todd Harbor to Pie Island in Canadian waters.

But the American Fur Company did change the face of the island during its glory days, but not through the fur trade. By the time they took over the fur was gone. They were quick with a backup plan to turn Isle Royale into a center of their subsidiary fishing operation. By the 1830s they had built stations at Grace Harbor, Duncan Bay, Belle Island, Merritt Island, and Rock Harbor, and a company headquarters at Checker Point. There's very little left of those sites, but back in my boyhood we knew these places and regularly saw and heard the old French Canadians who once lived there.

That's who the American Fur Company first brought here. These were voyageurs who had run out of fur work and became company boatmen and fishermen. They were the ones who caught the whitefish, lake trout, and siskiwit. They cleaned, salted, and transported these fish until the bottom fell out of the fish market. When I was a boy the old men of the island said that those voyageurs turned fishermen held celebrations in the interior uplands. They added that those spirits hung on up on Isle Royale's central hills and that the sounds of fiddle and concertina were heard in those spots late at night.

We have ghost ships here, too. Ones that served the island for a long time and can still be seen as phantoms in surrounding waters. There's the sloop *Madeline*, which visited each station to pick up the barreled fish. Then there were the schooners *William Brewster* and *Siskawit* which hauled the bulk cargoes of fish either to the Sault or to La Point down in Wisconsin. Those two vessels are sometimes seen in apparitions moored side by side in the island harbor.

The most significant presence of this type is the British schooner *Recovery*. The British actually used Isle Royale to hide the *Recovery* during the War of 1812. The Americans destroyed or captured all the other British ships on Lake Superior. It was covered with brush and allowed to freeze in over in McCargo Cove. It survived the war and went back to shuttling supplies between the Sault and Fort William. As long as there were American families living out here the *Recovery* would do taunting sunset cruises as an apparition on the Fourth of July.

I think that everything that ever touched this place comes back in some way. I can't explain it. But look at the artwork of island native Howard Sivertson back in Grand Portage, you can see that the spirit of those things hangs on for us. Everything from here comes back here. I know I expect to.

Ghosts of Steel

T he "Twin Ports" of Duluth and Superior occupy an unusual niche in my storytelling heart. My first visit to the area was over twenty years ago and coincided with a late winter blizzard. The storm forced a four-day unplanned stay at an "economy" motel and a prolonged penny ante poker game in the motel lobby. My fellow strandees were a motley crew of construction workers and sales representatives, with no small measure of anecdotes and obscure references dropped as crisply as the cards were dealt on the chipped formica table.

It was at that formica table that I first learned that the area represented a unique confluence of rail and lake travel, of northwoods and industrial culture, and of raw materials torn from the local ground and grown upon the prairies to the west. Those card players told me about the grain trade and of eastern Europe's ships hauling away Dakota wheat. They lectured me about taconite ore from the Mesabi range, hauled by rail, transferred to ships, and delivered up to the steel mills of Gary, Indiana, and Cleveland, Ohio. It seemed like they always came back to steel, steel rails, steel ore cars, steel grain cars, and steel ships.

The conversation provided background for a baker's dozen of subsequent Duluth visits over the years. There, in the harbor taverns and pool halls, I continued my education about the area's rich ethnic stew and struggle with nature. Out of these encounters first came a story called "Steaming Ore," which was published in a collection of Midwest railroad tales entitled Prairie Whistles. *The rough blue collar edges of that story created suspicion that there were more things to be heard from the burley men with windburned faces and large calloused hands who inhabited the local waterfront.*

However, it was not in a lakefarers' tavern that I heard my next tale. it was in the quiet of Duluth's Lake Superior Marine Museum, where the brawniness and violence of man's effort to eke out a living in this region is hinted at only obliquely. There I met Reginald and there he offered a raspy theory about what forces are unleashed when one dares to tear at the Earth.

*   *   *

Trains and ships and mines, men ripping at ore and cutting trees by the hundreds of thousands — that's what I see here in this commemoration of transportation. It was as if we were at war with our patch of God's Country. Like we were in a hurry to cut the big pines, get the iron out of the ground, crisscross the region with rails, and sail the lakes on our schedule, not Nature's. As in war there were casualties and many things done in the spirit of expediency.

Such things always leave scars. Scars on the body, the mind, the soul, and on the land itself. Scars stand for a healing of sorts, but also as a reminder of what we did. Maybe it's only for the bearers of scars to say whether they came by them honestly or righteously? Maybe it's only for more saintly fellows than I to say, "forgive them, they know not what they did?"

My people were all tied up in it, this ripping and tearing and rushing. All of them of my blood, Finn and Norwegian, Chippewa and Russian. In every damn part of it, from lumberjack to fisherman, from miner to railroader, and from dock worker to deck hand. All but the Chippewa side just tumbled into the region looking for a buck to feed hungry mouths. Nobody was thinking about anything else. Hell, there was country to build! We made things back then, we didn't launder each other's software!

A fellow gets older and he has room in his head and time on his hands to ponder such things. Did we do right by the place? Did we go a bit too fast? And then you wonder if we even have the ability to appreciate the consequences of a century's worth of ripping, tearing, and rushing.

I think I've thought of one angle that is starting to make sense to this old brain. It's from what I learned about the ghosts of steel. Not one ghost, but the type of things that come from the fighting and fussing of grubbing profit out of the land. Like the one ghost that wanders the docks since the time he was crushed by the ore cars.

See, these things we do here take a toll on men and machines. We've had strange deaths and unnoticed deaths. There have been men buried alive in grain, in the cars, in the elevators, and in the ship holds. Sometimes they're not found until they're dusty mummies. And the only things they leave behind are their ghosts who wander the dock and remind the living that life here is a lease, not a deed in perpetuity.

The ore docks have claimed their share, too. As you know, there's nothing like a winter day on the ore ducks. Slipping around on ice

up above the water, steam spraying out to loosen frozen loads in
the ore cars. It's a hard trade with balky cars, the insult of cold
metal on skin, and the lung-clogging red dust of taconite. That's
why you can see those wisps of men, ghosts in old work clothes out
at the old ore docks. Not just from the ones killed outright by in-
jury, but also the ones ground down by years of exposure to cold,
heat, steam, wind, and dust. Sometimes you can hear those wisps
of men hack the lungs, the ghostly reminder of what we called the
taconite cough. There were days when storms could push through
Duluth and raise red clouds of dust off of the hundreds and hundreds of hopper cars, like armies of wisps flying around and painting the town red to remind us of the blood shed while tearing at the
ground.

It was from those red dust storms that I figured out how haunted
we are here and how it came to be. The Chippewa in me knew that
you only take things out of the ground carefully and respectfully.
Like the way pipestone is quarried or the way that the old ones
took copper, in a sacred way. Then came the American push in the
Lake Superior country to rip out that copper. Nothing's been the
same since. Especially with the coming of the beasts of steel to do
the ripping, tearing, and hauling. A man with a pick, a horse, and
a wooden boat can only take so much. Give him heavy equipment,
trains, and steel ships and he can go wild. He can unleash spirits
stuck in the ground millions of years and lash his dead fellow workers to those spots. It's not a curse really, just an unease or imbalance
that comes with any disturbance to the order of natural things.

That's why these ghosts of steel converge here. Many were
claimed by steel here. Many others know it was the route that things
of steel take. The ore was pumped here like blood in the arteries of
rail, down from the pumping heart of the Mesabi Range. They
gave us the ghosts of Hibbing and Virginia. And they linked us in
a web of ore dock ghosts from here to Ashland and the Upper Peninsula.

They converge here courtesy of rail, off the prairies that probably should have never felt the steel plow. and out of forests lev-
eled with steel that are now nothing more than pulp farms. Plus
the yards, the railyards that groan with steel and the hundred year
legacy of men crushed by steel. Those places are as haunted as
anything I've ever seen.

Then the harbor! Anybody who can't find a ghost there has no
blood in their veins. Just look out the long stretch of Minnesota

Point. Look beyond the waves breaking on the piers at the bridge, out to where the deep water claimed the ships and men who trifled with her out of season. Sometimes I listen to those waves and hear the muffled last cries of those men who were still below when their great steel whales took the final dive to the bottom.

Some are far out past Minnesota Point. They litter the bottom from here to the Sault. Hell, from here to Kingston on Lake Ontario. You could rebuild New York with the steel on the bottom of these lakes. Well known ones like the *Edmund Fitzgerald* and many more lost to memory. But the ghosts of those crews wash up here. Must be the northeasters that push out this way.

Others got here in a more direct fashion. The *Mataafa* hit the piers in broad daylight and broke in two, putting nine men in the frigid waves to die. Look north across the channel to the Visitors Center. In a storm the ghosts of those nine still gather there.

Then there was the *Benjamin Noble*, lost in 1914. She was upbound from steel mills on Lake Erie, overloaded with railroad rails. She fought a heavy spring storm almost the whole way. One that just kept intensifying all the way across Lake Superior. It was a miracle that she even made it past Whitefish Point, double-loaded with rail and so low in the water that a drunk pissing on Saturday night could have sunk her. She made it all the way here, but could not find the channel because the storm had knocked the light out. She turned north, probably to make a run to Two Harbors. She disappeared into that storm, maybe to hit the banks off Knife Island. Anyway, the lake claimed all that rail and the entire crew, and not a speck of either ever turned up in this life. But those souls are down on that pier too, in the storms that throw the twenty foot spray.

So, yes, I think that when man claims the Earth and hammers it with steel it in turn claims him and hammers him with steel. This notion comes from every part of me, from Russian peasant, from Finnish socialist, from Norwegian farmer, and from Chippewa fisherman. But mostly it comes from what I've seen of these ghosts of steel. A life of that sort of thing drains the blood out of you. If you're to survive it, the blood must be replaced by steel.

Hell of a way to live!

Part V
Superior's South Shore

Spirit Lodge
of Wisconsin Point

S uperior, the city, always feels like home when I return from forays into Minnesota and Ontario. Two decades of attending meetings of labor unions and environmental groups will do that for you, especially when the local residents are solicitous and friendly. It is a blessing to be taken under wing by those devoted to the proposition that a familiarization with their city requires a visit to every cafe and tavern from the Bong airport to the Bong bridge to Allouez Bay. It seems each stop and spot has a story.

Many of the leads behind the tales of my earlier ghost story collection, Northern Frights, *came my way in the City of Superior. They made deep impressions on me because of the perspective and nature of the sources. These were urban blue collar people with deep connections to the land and the lakes. In a very real sense, it was the things the people of Superior told me about their hometown and the hometowns of their families that started me on the path to story collection. The same trip that left me snowbound in Duluth included a sojourn in Superior.*

It was in Superior that I first met city-dwelling members of the tribes of the Great Lakes. It was there that I received the first indication that Great Lakes stories were quite layered with the pain of the legacy of four hundred-plus years of cultural clash. The perspective of those sources was longer term than anything else I had previously discovered. The centuries of transition from French to English to American rule were seen by some of them as transitory aberrations, with even intertribal rivalries measured by multigenerational standards with roots in prehistory. This is excellent terrain for the story collector, for it is in such places that people understand the power of myth and the resonance of legend.

Superior drew me back many times over the next two decades. Stories of the logging days, the mining era, and of lakefaring were easy to come by. Most were lusty tales, filled with muscle and sweat. But I had begun to wonder if Superior had much in the way of supernatural lore. Then I met Misskwa in the Anchor Inn in Superior's warehouse district. He offered a theory about the pecking order of hauntings in this vicinity.

*   *   *

"Misskwa," is my lodge name. It means "Color of the South." It's not something I usually give out in taverns, but it goes with what I have to tell you about the spirit powers of this area. If you have been doing your homework, you know that every area has its own special energy and spirits. What people do in such places adds or subtracts to that energy in ways that they don't always appreciate.

In a very real sense the St. Louis River is where the Great Lakes begin. That has its own special power and problems. Some think that there were always magicians and sorcerers here. One Elder told me that it was a place of tricksters and shapeshifters even before humans came to this area. He even wondered if some of those places were meant to have people occupying them. That's how he felt about Minnesota Point and Wisconsin Point. Not that these places were the same back then, they shift with the currents and get built up and reshaped by humans.

That was his whole point, I think. The idea that those narrow bands of shifting land and water, their back bays and marshes, are not to be trifled with. There's something elemental about such places, like Earth being born or reborn in those places. As if they were meant only for lake birds to land on. It is to such places wizards and sorcerers always go to work up their magic and curses.

This Elder would not go out to Wisconsin Point for that reason. He felt that was where one old wizard long ago held a spirit lodge, with the intent of tapping energies that humans are not supposed to toy with. He felt that the impact of this black magic still lingers out there and that it could sap his energy. He worried that it could even trap his spirit out there if he wasn't careful.

Now you have to understand, this Elder has many ideas different than other Ojibwe traditionalists. He challenges some of the current Midewiwin[3] teachings and practices. He says that the true old ways are the ways of Seven Fires[4] that were preserved on the Ojibwe migration and brought to Madeline Island almost six hundred years ago after a journey of about five hundred years. And so those ways remained for over two hundred years, until the Europeans found their way up the Great Lakes. Things began to change almost immediately, and not for the better.

The combination of trade and politics accelerated the long-standing conflict with the Sioux. The Fond du Lac Ojibwe, my people, settled here along the St. Louis River after those wars with the Sioux.

French traders came, then the British with the Northwest Company and their fort. The old ways were threatened. With the British came the diseases. We had four epidemics of smallpox in the late 1700s and early 1800s. Not only was the loss of life horrific, it altered how we as a people functioned.

The British traders did not like dealing with the clan leaders and the old medicine men, who stressed traditional obligations to provide for the young and the old. Such obligations ran against the extended absences required by trade. With the people weakened, the British resorted to the practices of conferring chiefdoms on those they could control. An underground sprang up in opposition to this that took some of the Midewiwin traditions from the Chequamegon Ojibwe and reorganized it like a secret society. It was like one part Masonic order, with degrees, one part church hierarchy, with priests, and one part Anishinabe spiritual tradition.

It was in this environment that the local wizard set up shop and was said to conduct a spirit lodge in the Wisconsin Point area. The Elder told me that this wizard crossed over from healthy spiritual practice into the black magic of curses and even magical assassinations with symbolic arrows. So instead of healing and comforting, as in the Chequamegon tradition, the wizard practiced something more like voodoo. And it weakened the British and hastened their departure from the area.

This spirit lodge was supposed to be the place where all sorts of spirits could be summoned and be put to work for bad purposes. Spirits of earlier wizards could be revived here. The dead could be made to walk and carry out orders. Somehow the wizard was able to harness the underlying power of the lake and pervert it. As a result he became a powerful man, and those of the tribe in the fur trade would pay him exorbitant fees in order to suppress their competitors and eliminate their rivals. It served as kind of a redistribution of wealth scheme. I guess that's a common undercurrent in religious cult scams.

Well, the wizard eventually was ostracized by more reputable Midewiwin priests. The Elder told me that they fought magical battles with the corrupt wizard to keep his power confined to this area. Then he eventually passed on and the United States came to control the area. The Fond du Lac Ojibwe mostly retreated into Minnesota and the story was almost forgotten. Except that every generation had an elder or two who knew the story and could warn tribal itinerants, like myself, to steer clear of such things.

So I've been learning such things from the Elder. He wants me to study with him and take up his brand of old Chequamegon Midewiwin teachings. I don't know about that. He wants me to give up the beer. He's not one hundred percent against drinking, he just doesn't like the smell of beer sweat in the sweat lodge. He says it smells like a tavern urinal. He wants me to go back to the old ways of the vision quest and the drum trance, to travel as a spirit and see other worlds.

He has taught me many things about that spirit lodge on Wisconsin Point. He sends me out there sometimes on his errands. I know that must seem strange considering all the scary stuff he says about it. I've come to view it as a long term danger, like a radioactive waste site. But the Elder tells me to have a few beers before I go and that the spirit of the wizard will just think I'm one of the stupid drunks that wander out there.

What I do is leave objects out there that are connected to other bad situations. The Elder does things like exorcisms and if he can find something that has a connection to an annoying spirit that's bothering someone, well, you get that object out to Wisconsin Point. Then the power of the old wizard and the spirit lodge take over and they suck the haunting right out of the troubled place and pull it into the spirit lodge.

It's kind of funny how that works. Something that was created for evil can be put to use for good. I guess a lot of medicines are poison in the wrong amount. I heard that the Elder coaxed a ghost off the *S.S. Meteor* at Barkers Island. But he won't tell me the details of such things. He just sends me out on Wisconsin Point with jars, pots, and little bundles and tells me not to look inside. So I don't. He also tells me not to try to find the exact spot of the spirit lodge. He said that ordinarily a person could step right on it and nothing would happen. On the other hand, if you're on a mission of spirit, then that wizard's power will suck you right into that lodge and you won't get out without the intervention of an army of medicine men.

The Elder wants me to be as a child out there. He likes to insult me and tells me he picked me because I'm simple-minded to begin with. He warns me not to get too big for my britches and never, never try to tap the power of the lake. He tells me over and over that the lesson of the wizard and the spirit lodge is to respect the power of the lake. If you respect it, then it will come to you in a good way. If not, then you'll just get pulled into a dead end like that spirit lodge.

How did he put it? Oh yeah, his view on seeking power was, "You don't stick your head in a toilet or your arm in a garbage disposal to see how they work."

Ghoul of the Brule

Wisconsin outdoorsmen have a long acquaintance with the Brule River in eastern Douglas County. Generations of hunters, fishermen, and hikers have explored this river of many moods as it courses its winding way from the marshy upland portage with the St. Croix River to the mouth on the shore of Lake Superior. Storied encounters with bear, trout, and wolves have been handed down since the pinery days. Today the old tales are leavened with a mixture of contemporary family day trips, kayak passages, and ATV incursions.

Those familiar with the area simply call it "the Brule," referring to the river, the state forest, the watershed area, and, perhaps, the state of mind that is associated with time spent in any or all of these. For many, a trip to the Brule represents a journey into an unusual mixture of terrain and flora. It is one of those areas that exerts a long term hold over those who visit it for reasons that are not entirely apparent. When questioned, fans of the Brule often mention the "feel."

Part of the feel has to do with the strange experiences that locals and visitors alike seem to find with some frequency. One does not have to search for long to hear stories about animals acting strangely or odd lights sparkling in the pools of the river. Finally, the Brule is somewhat of a magnet for odd personalities who delight in conveying a creepy sensibility.

These characters can appear out of nowhere at the oddest places and times, whether one is beachcombing near the mouth of the Brule or flyfishing the headwaters. Such types seem to be mostly scruffy strangers, middle-aged or older, who seem to materialize out of thin air and strike up conversations as if they were lifelong friends.

Burl was one such erstwhile companion who gave me a half hour of monologue before he slipped away in a canoe. He rendered his narrative in a sing-song verse that I have heard occasionally further south in the Mississippi valley (most notably in the tale "Wyalusing Snake Man" in Giants in the Land.*) The spot was the boatlanding on Brule River Road, a half mile upstream from the lake. By the time he left I was as surprised and confused as he was.*

*   *   *

Ghoul of the Brule, eh, Ghoul of the Brule, the creature's haunted many a pool from the head of the Brule to the bones at the bottom of the lake what were Paddy O'Doul. It's a jewel of a ghoul, spawned here on the Brule, what makes its own rules for the pools of the Brule and sits like a mugwump on a lake bottom stool. When it rises from that throne of a stool, to act out ghoul rules, it roils up Lake Superior's azul and shakes all the pools from the mouth of the river to the head of the Brule.

He what fools with the Ghoul of the Brule is but a pitiful, pitiful fool. To pick a fight with the Ghoul of the Brule leaves no doubt you've the brain of a mule. A look at the face of the Ghoul of the Brule, whether face to face or reflected by glassy pool, is enough to make mortal fools into imbeciles what drools. I've seen the pitiful faces of those fools what wander from the mouth of the river to the head of the Brule. It's but an act of mercy when the Ghoul of the Brule drags them down in a pool, hauls their flesh down in the deep to cool, then gnaws on their bones out by Paddy O'Doul's.

It's hard to fathom the rules of ghouls, especially our very own Ghoul of the Brule. For what is a ghoul and what are the rules what govern these ghouls that lurk in pools whilst waiting for fools? Our American ghoul comes from the French *goul*, which farther back descends from the Arabic *ghul*, what makes the Ghoul of the Brule a thing as old as the Old Norse Thul. It is said the ghoul, to be considered a ghoul, must regularly feast on the flesh of a fool. For if not fed this diet of fools the creature will lose the powers what belong to ghouls.

As to what be ghouls, there are alternative schools. Don't be asking them what drools or those who be fools. No, the oldest school, that of the Arabian *ghul*, sees a flesh eating demon in each and every ghoul. But that Arabian ghul over desert does rule and knows nothing of the lake's deep cool and the head of the Brule. Now the French goul is closer to American ghoul, but is confined to graveyards by musty old rules. Our Ghoul of the Brule is of the deep cool and of the shimmering pools.

So here we operate on Lake Superior's rules, which overrule even ghouls and tell fish where to school. For the lake lets a ghoul play fast and loose with the usual rules. Thus the Ghoul of the Brule can look like a beautiful woman to a fool at the side of a shimmering pool, appear as a horrible serpent to the imbecile who drools, and be Davey Jones himself out by the bones of Paddy O'Doul.

So what the hell is the Ghoul of Brule? Damn if I know, they don't teach that in school. Be it half-Indian by breed from the first people of the Brule or be it something cobbled together by Finns wielding tools? Be it a ghost of the Brule or zombie of the pools or something of the ooze out in the deep cool?

It's not something to be measured by the scientist's joule. It's a mite like the feathered poullard if your vision be dual and you don't look very hard. If we killed it, would local oologist be prompted to eulogy? Or would a general zoologist talk of its duality? Its face is odd, inlaid with bone like art of the boulle, its hide is as carpet from old Kabul. It sleeps in the rock shafts known as moulin, it snores like a chainsaw, yep, no fooling.

To catch the Ghost of Brule would require vast tools and demand of man cast iron jewels. But be your name Jules, endowed with such tools to fight daring duels, you'd find yourself wealthy at Yule as a rule. If you be Jules, possessed of metal family jewels, make your own rules and gather a treasure vast as the jewels of the old King of Thul.

Be you not Jules, be just an ordinary fool with brain soaked in his drool, you'll not have a prayer against the Ghoul of Brule. You'll not get a chance to cheer boolah, boolah over the moolah, moolah. You'll just be fuel for the Ghoul's cesspool. You'll just be dead Mulligan for the hooligan doing the hula down in the hull again. For only a Jules can conquer this ghoul and rid all the pools from the head of the Brule to Superior's deep cool. Be your name English Poole, or Boole, French Toule or Joule, German Buhl or Muhl, even a stout Irish O'Toole or devout Muslim Abdul, You'll end up a bone pile next to Paddy O'Doul.

I can see by your eyes that you be not Jules, my eyes tell me you've not the right tools and not the right heft or hardness of jewels. So leave this place, you outsider fool and vacate the country that lines the cruel Brule. Don't fish in the pools that dot the cold Brule. Don't paddle the rapids in defiance of rules. Don't swim at the mouth where the sleek splake school. Just go back to your farm country and harness your mules, forget you've ever seen the river of jewels, and if you're damn lucky your dreams will not rule with sight and sound of the Ghoul of the Brule.

Were you about to say something?

Spectral Lights of Port Wing

Highway 13 in Wisconsin takes the traveler through varied biological and cultural terrain. Stories are abundant all along its three hundred mile course, from Superior to Wisconsin Dells. This was a classic touring road in the heady days after World War II, when heavy sedans pulled gleaming airstream trailers. Urban residents experienced most of rural Wisconsin along Highway 13, from holsteins to pine plantations to ore docks. But many travelers from that era told me that their favorite portion of that tour was the Highway 13 "Hook" that bends this northbound road northeast from Ashland, around Red Cliff and then west to Port Wing.

Many of the "flatlander" tourists found this area a Great Lakes version of New England, with taciturn residents of small fishing villages, stoic natives in forest fastnesses, and burly lumberjacks. Similarities between the two areas may exist in the realm of stereotypes. However, at ground level, among the people of this particular piece of Great Lakes shoreline, one finds very little in the way of New England puritanism. Indeed there is a rollicking side to the local culture that seems to clash with the outsider's vision of placid life. From aged Finns rolling naked in the snow after saunas to young Ojibwe men slapping bear rumps for sport to auto races on lake ice, there is little held back in the way of impulse here.

Such tendencies make the story collector's job easier. In perhaps two dozen journeys around the Hook, I found little need for extractive interview techniques or eavesdropping. Rather, it was often the case that total strangers would unburden incredible tales on me without any prompting whatsoever. It was those sources who taught the lessons of storytelling as a statement of grievances. Later I would come to discover that this is, perhaps, a subgenre of stories that can be found in the Wisconsin northwoods. They are generally tinged with conspiratorial thinking, hardship, and no small amount of anger. The tellers of such things do not equivocate, they offer no alternate theories nor do they couch their stories in cautious terms. They know and understand what they saw.

The first time I encountered such conviction was nearly twenty years ago in Port Wing. The occasion was a fundraiser barbecue near a baseball diamond. A weatherbeaten face shaded by a vintage Milwaukee Braves cap plopped down across from me at the plank table. He talked while I ate my chicken. After he left, someone at the table said, "well, that's a new one for Old Kinney."

* * *

You're not from the Department of Natural Resources are you? Or the federal fishing and wildlife people? Damn if I'd share a table with those potlickers. Well, I can tell you ain't one of them, cause I can smell what you got in that coffee mug there. I'm just on the suspicious side because I saw the lights last night. What the old geezers use to call the "spectral lights." You know, lights of a spirit nature. That makes them different from the other north country lights that you find over in the Upper Peninsula or up in Canada or down by that Navy radio transmitter. That stuff is either government experiments or UFOs. No, these spectral lights have a long tradition of living in proximity to humans and a man can read their language if he puts his mind to it.

Back in the old countries they called it *ignis fatuus*, or foolish fire. I looked that up in a book after one old boy told me it meant "lit farts." But the principle is the same in both definitions, a common sense view that this is a thing that you're better off not pursuing or trying to catch in a bottle. But this caution only applies to trying to chase spectral lights, not to trying to understand them or use them to your benefit.

You see these things exist all over the world or at least they did at one time. Every culture that had people out and about hunting, fishing, farming, working timber, or snatching gull eggs had something like this. But I think those things slip away as people disappear indoors, and stare into electronic screens, and dream up such things as fuzzy covers for toilet seat lids. But that's how it goes, a man loses touch with things of this Earth if he forgets the sensations of whizzing in the wind and taking a dump in a stump. Where spectral lights go after we're declawed and spayed is an entirely open question.

But for now we still got them around here, Praise the Big Guy. We got them in ways that tip us off when the government snoops come round. Kind of our early warning system. And the Big Guy sure knows we have our share of problems with those chuckleheads, federal and state. Have you heard of their little sting deal that they're running up here? It's Operation Gillnet or Gullnuts or something like that, according to their blabbermouth informants. The governments says that they're trying to stop illegal fishing, but it's a deeper agenda than that. Everyone along this lake knows that they're out to end commercial fishing for good.

It will happen in another generation anyway and the spectral lights will leave here as they have thousands of fishing villages where the tourist army demands unconditional surrender. You see, we're in the way of charter sports fishing. It seems like that industry has more clout with the powers that be than us working stiffs who haul nets. It seems that some lard butt who comes up from the cities and pops a couple hundred bucks must be guaranteed his catch of fish, the hell with our livelihoods and generations of fishing tradition.

I heard these snoops already have entrapped a pile of commercial fishermen and are using them to catch the rest of us and pull our licenses. Then the sports cruisers, with their box lunches, will have the run of the lake. Maybe a few Indians will hang on, if they win their treaty case. Otherwise it will be the end of hauling nets and making market with a good catch. But I plan to go on my own schedule and use the lights to keep myself clear of the snoops.

These spectral lights have been a lot of things in a lot of places, especially if there's water and boats involved. Each culture had a slightly different meaning and a slightly different origin. The Swedes say that the lights are the souls of unbaptized children. Finns say that they are the spirits of hunting dogs. To the Germans they are spirit entities unto themselves called Irrlicht. Norwegians see them over land as harbingers of soon to come funeral processions. English call them Will-O'-the-Wykes and consider them ill omens.

This name thing is all over the place. I've heard old Indians call them fire creatures. An old Russian over by Cornucopia called them witchfire. Then I've heard them called corpse candles, torch of the dead, travelers' lights, jenny burntails, johnny lanterns, woods lamps, and kit-in-the-candlesticks. Among the impatient you'll even hear things like "flaming whatchamacallit."

Locally we have the tradition of the spectral lights leading people astray. But what knothead follows a light around anyway. Lights are signals, right? Like Paul Revere watching across Boston harbor for one if by sea, two if by land. Or was it the other way around? The one of my blood who taught me to mend nets and smell weather told me that the lights signal that things are out of balance. He told me that spectral lights by great bodies of water emanate from special stones. Such rocks can be found as submerged cairns, buried megaliths, or inconspicuous boulders camouflaged in pebble rubble. He said that the Vikings installed such a device here, but declined to point it out to me.

I've learned that this was a common enough ancient technology among people along the North Sea. Apparently the Irish and Scots used them as warning lights at various times in their tormented histories. The lights have a sense of alien presences and hostile intent. Or, as it was handed down to me, they've got a nose for imbalance, like a miner's canary.

All I know is that when I see the lights I've learned to take a low profile for a few days. That's advice straight out of North Sea smuggler lore. But it works for me and I haven't been pinched yet. In the last few years it almost always turns out that if I've seen the lights there will be later confirmations that snoops are on the prowl or that thieves are working the area.

Whoa, I see a suspicious truck pulling into the lot. See it? Crew cab, no rust, no mud, four clean-shaven faces, and four fresh haircuts. That would be either missionaries or snoops. I'm betting on the latter. Keep an eye out tonight. Look west to Quarry Point and you'll have even odds after midnight of seeing those spectral lights. Give the boys in the truck my regards. I'm moving on.

Spirit Well of Sand Island

Twenty-two clumps of land make up the archipelago known as the Apostle Islands. The French tendency to name geographic features after religious figures and events demonstrates that church-controlled education emphasized scriptures at the expense of earthly mathematics. Spirit lore and incidents of odd happenings in the Apostle Islands could almost account for a story collection of its own, with hefty amounts coming from the only currently settled isle in the chain, Madeline Island. Stories in the area range in time from the modern urban legends of tourists to echoes of the paleolithic.

Prior story collecting efforts in the area produced three representative tales in my 1998 work, **Northern Frights.** *One of those tales, "The Old One," dealt with the earliest confrontations between Lake Superior and humans. There one finds a theme that surfaces again and again in Lake Superior lore: the deep soulful power of the lake. The terms used are reverential, even when not overtly spiritual, and reverberate with mystery. The earliest encountered name, Gitchi Gummi, sounds like a spirit presence unto itself.*

Not surprisingly, Apostle Island lighthouses occupy a substantial niche in the cumulative lore of the area. The lights became indispensable to navigation as the shipping traffic grew and as vessels became larger. As noted in earlier stories involving lighthouses, the isolated environments of these light stations and the personalities of those who manned them acted as a virtual guarantee that strange accounts would emerge from this subculture. Lake Superior lighthouses were not exceptions to this rule, indeed they often offered more rigors than light stations elsewhere.

Emily is a living repository of such lore. She is a self-educated expert in the history and legends of the eight Apostle Island lights. But her real attachment is to the Sand Island Light. There she served a stint as a volunteer lightkeeper and still occasionally helps out at the Ranger Station. Though up in years, she was still able to lead the way on the two-mile walk to Sand Island Light and sound enough of wind to share her story on the way.

*   *   *

People in places like this understand the power of water. It's an omnipresent thing, inside our bodies and even beneath the desert sands. When people get close to a thing as powerful as Lake Superior they lose sight of the subtleties, the small ways in which water works. If you think about it, there's a unity to all of water on Earth. It's all been part of a greater whole at one time, and every isolated drop is likely to come back to that oneness again.

There was a story told out here at one time about how the power of Lake Superior could be felt upon the land. In the times that the story was told, we had a village out here on Sand Island, a place called East Bay, where boats still dock. A lively little community in those times, with social events and fiddle music floating on the air, and now barely a trace left that it existed. East Bay was a village filled with yarns and tall tales. It's what people did to occupy time, especially in the winter. Most of those yarns were just for fun, but there were a few that were drawn out of the instincts of East Bay residents.

Of those serious topics, questions relating to the Sand Island Light were a major focus. Though only two miles north from East Bay, there was a different feel to the point where the old lighthouse rose above the rocks. Maybe it was because the old lighthouse was the most impressive structure on the island, a brownstone in the style of the Normandy coast. Maybe it was the odd series of lighthouse inhabitants, who often kept to an isolated light station regimen even though they were within easy walking distance of East Bay. Even after the light was automated, the succession of lighthouse tenants proved a strange lot.

I was born around the time of the switch from lighthouse keepers to seasonal tenants. So I have heard of the lightkeepers but I did not know them personally. But during my East Bay childhood even the lightkeepers of the 1880s were recalled in minute detail. And it was thought that there was something a bit off about all of them. It was said that none of them, despite some lengthy tenure, were suited to lighthouse duty. Apparently they were all easily bored and prone to bouts of loneliness and depression.

This is where the stories of the old lighthouse well come into play. The oldest men on the island recalled that a shallow well was dug out there and hit a spring of pure water. This is where accounts diverge. Some say that the well was simply masonry placed over a natural spring-fed pit that had long served natives and explorers. Others said it was totally a man-made reservoir and that, for convenience sake, the lighthouse was built over it. A few insist that the well was slightly inland from the lighthouse, down a long forgotten path. Those accounts then converge again in agreement that the well was the source of mischief and was sealed up as a preventive measure against further mishap.

Those who believed in the antiquity of this well said that those who drank from it were lured by irresistible forces to sleep the final sleep in the waters of Lake Superior. Those who thought the well of more recent origin had the experience of lightkeeper Lederle to point to. He was the first lightkeeper and was rumored to wish for more stimulation at his isolated outpost. As such solitary figures are apt to do, he took to mumbling his desires aloud. Then, apparently, one day he voiced his wish for something to break the tedium while leaning over the well. Supposedly, within twenty-four hours the *Prussia*, a sturdy steamboat, caught fire within his sight and he was occupied with hours of rescue efforts and weeks of inquiry sufficient to get him through another winter. No other evidence of Lederle's abuse of the well has been handed down. Though some suspect that the law of unintended consequences was quite operative and brought misfortune to Lederle. The oldest of East Bay's residents were purposely silent on the particulars.

After Lederle, came a man called Luick who was perhaps even more ill-suited to the task of tending the light. It was said that he was victim to chronic melancholia. Some thought that he put the well to good use and managed to wed a young outgoing woman who was industrious and quick of mind. What else but a charm would get such a woman to go to a lighthouse? She stayed on with Luick for ten increasingly unhappy years. I was told that Luick used the well to wish her off the island and she never returned.

But Luick was apparently the marrying kind and went to the well and the altar a second time. That was about five or six years after his first wife's departure. No one was surprised by that second marriage or the possibility that the well produced another catch better than Luick's net would merit. What struck most with a memory of those times was what happened shortly after the first Mrs. Luick left Sand Island. I'm referring to the wreck of the *Sevona*, one of the biggest and sturdiest ships of the early 1900s.

The loss of the *Sevona* is one of those freak occurrences fraught with mystery. A very sturdy ship, with an extremely capable crew, fell prey to the type of disaster that the Sand Island Light was meant to prevent. It was a very strange storm that hit the Apostle Islands in that early September long ago. Those who remembered it said it started out like a tropical typhoon, interspersed with waterspouts and apple-size hail, and ended with a temperature plunge and freezing rain. Only such bizarre conditions could account for the *Sevona* hitting the shoal only a bit more than a mile from the point without seeing the light.

The *Sevona* broke up on that shoal within minutes. The captain and a good portion of the crew perished. Luick recorded the disaster in the Sand Island Lighthouse log, though no overt rescue effort was noted. Luick did, however, aid in the recovery of bodies. More than one old fisherman in East Bay thought of the well and wondered what Luick had said to it.

It was after Luick and the sealing of the well that the story takes a different twist. By the time the government was renting out the Lighthouse as a cottage there was a feeling that the lighthouse was haunted. But no one linked the haunting to the dead of the *Sevona* or to Luick's dead children. It was a different kind of haunting presence.

East Bay of that time had elderly people who knew about such things. They told me about spirit wells and their properties and the power of water. One old Norwegian lady was particularly knowledgeable. She said that all bodies of water are spirit abodes and that each body has its own individual spirit. Some are guardians, some are tricksters, and others are clearly malignant. The problem, as she saw it, was that we had lost the old knowledge of how to deal with such spirits. She said that ancient people had precise rituals for propitiating water spirits with offerings and sacrifices.

She saw wells as passageways for water spirits, in this case the Lake Superior Spirit. She said that the well was too close to the lake, that you never build over a well or, worse yet, try to seal one without the proper ritual. Sealing a well will aggravate water spirits, and make them aggressive in seeking out other routes. For her it was just a hop, skip, and a jump to the matter of wishing wells and the misuse of such power. She talked of the long forgotten counterpart to the wishing well, the cursing well, and speculated on whether or not there was a real difference between the two. Not to mention the healing wells and the divining wells. But perhaps the desire to cure or to see the future are simply other forms of wishes. In any event, she said that such wells almost always become either holy shrines or shunned places.

So perhaps it's for the best that the exact location of the spirit well of Sand Island is lost to us. If it indeed is directly tapped into the powerful presence of Lake Superior then it might be too strong for pampered modern humans. The old lady of East Bay said that such things reveal themselves again only to the arrogant who need a lesson and to humble seekers who are pure of heart.

Red Cliff
Sweat Lodge Encounter

The Red Cliff Ojibwe loom larger in Anishinabe affairs than their relatively small numbers would suggest. In part this can be attributed to their links to the Anishinabe migration traditions which depict nearby Madeline Island as the destination of that mass movement of people. It is at Red Cliff where the stories of Chief Buffalo, the last of the great Ojibwe traditional chiefs, are kept fresh in the memories of young tribal members. Contemporary Red Cliff has also produced more than its share of political activists, educators, and artists who have shaped cultural images and agendas.

Perhaps the best known of these recent cultural ambassadors is the late Walt Bresette, who had a totally modern view of communications wedded to a deep and intense Anishinabe spiritual view. There are few American Indians who touched as many non-Indians in a heartfelt way as Walt. He was a master storyteller and had a way of filling rooms with light and laughter. On one hand he was an abrasive activist who could be strident on behalf of treaty rights and in defense of the sanctity of the waters of Lake Superior. On the other hand he had an immense capacity for warmth and was fond of "adopting" entire auditorium audiences into his tribe.

Walt also engineered many Ojibwe cultural encounters for non-American-Indian friends and served as a mentor for many young spiritual seekers. He sometimes referred to himself as a wizard, but in ways that left his audience wondering if he was using the term as political metaphor or as storytelling device. No matter what the circumstances, he was visibly amused by the quizzical looks of proteges in the wake of strange or ambiguous events. Some thought that he only had to mention a totem and a living specimen would appear. He told others of dreams involving them and then the circumstances described would later come to pass. He professed no knowledge of how such things worked in practical or esoteric terms. He would simply shrug his shoulders and chuckle.

Among those who were launched into such experiences by Walt is Scott, an environmental activist who now focuses on anti-mining campaigns in the upper Midwest. His foray into the confines of a traditional sweat lodge was initially casual, but soon turned to the inexplicable.

*   *   *

When I was invited to the sweat lodge I thought of it as a sauna with a little bit of superstition and ceremony thrown in. Was I in for a surprise! You know, I'm a little leery of non-Indians latching on to Indian ceremonies, but I was asked and that made it different. I went to be polite. Wasn't that very white of me?

My first response inside was a kind of a stiffness of disposition. I felt out of place. Sitting naked, butt to butt with a bunch of men you don't know is not exactly an icebreaker. And I just couldn't read their expressions in the dimness. In the poor light their looks ranged from blank to grimaces to glowering to maniacal. My face probably went through all those options in the time I was in there.

The Naganwa[5] was very good about explaining the lodge and its purpose. He put me at ease a little at first, when I was still of the mind that he was functioning on the level of allegory or parable. But I soon woke up to the fact that everything he said he meant literally. That got my ass twitching in the cedar boughs on the lodge floor. Plus, I soon learned there is no such thing among the Ojibwe as a short story. Gosh, those guys can be longwinded.

Our Naganwa first told the migration story, then the story of the medicines of cedar, sage, and tobacco. Then he really got warmed up with the story of the drum and how it was the heartbeat of the world. That turned out to be a short preface compared to the saga of the pipe that followed. But even that was nothing compared to the epic of the sweat lodge that was his real object. As he told the story of the sweat lodge it seemed like he needed to resort to the voices and personas of about two dozen human characters and virtually half the animal kingdom. It felt long enough a time to grow a beard.

I can distill it down to something that will only take a few minutes. Our Naganwa said the sweat lodge was brought to the Ojibwe by a boy on his first vision quest by the lake. His fast gave him a vision of the Seven Grandfathers of the Anishinabe, the very ones who prompted the migration. The boy was expected because of a prophecy and the Grandfathers greeted him and gave him a gift of a purifying ceremony to be taken back to the Ojibwe. It was the gift of the sweat lodge.

The Grandfathers were very precise in their instructions to the boy. It had to be built in a certain way and the site had to be prepared in a certain way. It's to be made from willow saplings and has an actual door in the East and symbolic doors in the other directions. In the center of the lodge is the pit that represents the womb of Mother Earth. It is in this pit that the hot stones are placed. Participants are seated in a particular way, with the Naganwa's helpers sitting in the four directions and the Oshkabays[6] sitting where they are told.

It soon got insufferably hot in there, with intense steam when water was poured on the rocks. It made me want to get closer to the cool ground, to nestle right into those cedar boughs. But there's no room to do so, unless you're willing to be under someone's crack. This is when you start to get woozy and the Naganwa's voice starts to sound hypnotic. He talked about how this lodge is a return to the womb, how it is a return to the fires of Creation, and how the humble crawl out at the end is rebirth. He talked about how it is possible within the lodge to see things one wouldn't ordinarily see and travel out of one's body to distant places.

In the beginning of the experience I could concede such possibilities only as the mind-altering effects of the heat. But as more stones were added and more steam was made I started to reconsider this issue. The water poured by the Naganwa on the hot rocks started to come alive for me as he invoked its Lake Superior source. I started to feel the rhythm of the lake swells right in that lodge, felt the crash of the lake upon Red Cliff's rocky shores as the water was poured into the pit, and felt the steam as lake mist that can envelope land and water in a white blanket.

At that point I wasn't hot anymore. Everything I ever thought about boundaries between fact and supernatural went out the window at that point. In that sweat lodge I came to see how the Red Cliff Ojibwe came to be on intimate terms with the lake, how what seem like mysteries are just confusion created by our sense of boundaries. The lodge let me feel the lake in me and through that feeling I came to drop the separateness between myself and the lake. In that moment I felt that I was a part of everything and that everything was a part of me. My European sense of time finally went out the window and opened perceptual doors for me that I had never imagined could exist.

The things I saw after that are hard to fathom. I thought for a time that we were afloat on Lake Superior, even storm-tossed for a time, and my ears filled with the howl of a great wind. Then it seemed like I was under the surface of the lake, down in a deep place where one could encounter the spirit entities that dwell in Lake Superior. There I met beings that talked to me; old Ojibwe medicine men, American sailors, and even Vikings. Even creatures that had something to tell me, from giant sturgeons to grinning cousins of the Loch Ness monster. It would be hard to explain their messages and, besides, the Naganwa said such things were meant for me alone.

Down in that deep place I even saw long gone people from my family. They were so soothing and I took great comfort from what I felt was a blessing from them on my Earth-healing and Earth-protecting work. Before the lodge I felt edgy and angry over my environmental work. After that time in the lodge I am at peace with those efforts. It's no longer about getting even or fighting powerful interests. It's about doing right, living right, and feeling that connection to the water, the rocks, and everything.

When I came out of that lodge the cool air filled my lungs like a baby's first breath, shocking and exhilarating. I even cried. I felt a connection to that air, a familiarity with every molecule that passed through the lungs of everything since the first breath. Then we dove into lake Superior and felt that clash and electricity of the power of opposites. Heat and cold meeting within the body and soul to cause an alertness and aliveness that ties everything together and makes sure you're back in the real world.

Some of my friends sense the change in me since my visit to the sweat lodge. Some of them make fun of it, others respect it even though they don't understand it. I'm not sure I understand it. A few friends keep asking me what I saw in there. So I tell them the basics, that I saw spirits. I sometimes even walk them through the distinctions between the ghosts of people and the entities that are not from the ordinary world.

But I almost never tell anybody the most important thing I saw during my sweat lodge encounter. It's not easy to explain how that sweat lodge let me follow a drop of water from the primordial oceans to the ice age glaciers to the clouds to the rain to the fluids within me and back to Lake Superior. How do you explain being able to see yourself in every drop of water?

Bad River Spirit Bear

The distance between Red Cliff and the state line shared with Michigan's Upper Peninsula is not significant in terms of linear space. But I found it hard to cover the span without resorting to one more story. Where to start? Red Cliff itself offered a good supply that could easily merit a berth. Then there are a good two dozen from the Apostle Islands unpopulated isles. Madeline Island, with its impressive cultural and historical legacies, is almost a book in itself. Windblown Washburn and beautiful Bayfield both have tales resonating in the rocks of their shorelines. Ashland's saga is ripe with the specters of timber, rail, and lake. One is convinced during even a short sojourn along Chequamegon Bay that this area has sufficient lore, be it maritime or classic northwoods, to fill a lengthy collection.

Thus when it came time to translate two decades of snippets recorded on cafe napkins, beer coasters, and motel stationery into a manuscript I was faced with tough decisions. Out of the multitude suggested by my rough field notes, I decided to revisit one more Chequamegon narrative before passing to the east. Picking among them was the problem. Then I remembered the general advice about folkways given to me by livestock buyer and homesteading mentor Robert White, "Stick with what sticks to your ribs." It was a useful reminder that some things call us more than we recall them.

Within that advice was a clear answer and a vivid memory. The place was the Bad River Reservation. The time was the mid-1980s, the beginning of the big flareup over the treaty rights claims made by the various tribes of the Lake Superior Ojibwe. Just as at Red Cliff, the circumstances were engineered by the late Walt Bresette. Here at Bad River he introduced me to a host of technicians and wildlife managers in the employ of the Great Lakes Indian Fish and Wildlife Commission. They in turn put me into the hands of Burdette, a repository of knowledge he described as "wildcrafting." But his wisdom went beyond physical skills; he was in touch with everything that mattered to him.

* * *

We'll canoe out into some of the sloughs. There you can find the essence of the place. There's a mixture here of the worlds of water and land. So much of Lake Superior shoreline is a black and white thing. There on one side you've got land, hard as granite. On the other side of the foamy line you've got the muscle of Lake Superior beating against the rock and slowly winning the battle. Here at Bad River it's a different kind of line that you find between the worlds of water and land. The line is more blurred. Maybe if the lake is winning elsewhere, it's losing here or at least settling for a draw, with the sand throwing up bars and the mud filling the back bays. Here the land makes the inland waters snake through marsh before allowing them to join their kin in the lake.

This is a place more like you'd find in a bayou or delta. Much of it doesn't fit in the category of water or land. It's an in-between place and it's important to understand it as such and learn from it. You do that by watching and listening to the things that live in such places. Different things live in such places, and even the usual things live in different ways in such places.

There's a gentleness to be found in this place and a sense of secrets, too. Some places get to you with their forcefulness and how they jump out at you. Places like this make you be more mindful, make you watch more closely for small things and signs that are easy to miss. My old Great Grand called them gifts, presences, and forces. That's what he said I would find in the in-between of water and land. Of course, that's what brought the Ojibwe to the area in the first place, the prophecy of a gift. That was the promise of food that grows on water, the wild rice that created the sense of abundance and surplus that brought an end to the wandering.

The presences are in those small things that signal the coming and passing of seasons. Things that delight the eye and remind us of beauty. The forces are in the big things that remind us of the power that lives in our Mother the Earth. Things that touch the spirit and connect us to the Great Spirit.

Then there are things that are meant for each of us alone. These are gifts, presences, and forces all at the same time. Such things bring us wisdom, mindfulness, and healing if we are open to their lessons. I have such a thing that I found out in this in-between world when I was young. Something that my Great Grand told me that I would find, a thing from his vision. It is a Spirit Bear.

Now bears are unique beings to begin with and have a special place in spirit matters. But not every bear is a Spirit Bear. No, a

Spirit Bear does things that ordinary bears cannot do and helps you in ways that regular bears cannot. Sometimes a bear is just a bear. But sometimes it's a teacher and a helper. If such a bear comes into your life then you are marked for a different path and you cannot escape it.

When I was young, 6 or 7 years old, I started to dream of bears, something that Great Grand said would shape my life. He was right. At ten, I was picking thimbleberries down near the beach when I got between a mother bear and her cubs. She rushed me and pushed me, leaving these claw scars on my neck. She was about to swat my head off when a big boar bear growled and ran her off. He gave me a look that made me feel like I knew him.

After that I had protective medicine and got an early start on hunting and other adult pursuits. It got me through two tours in Vietnam, twenty-five years in law enforcement, and plenty of out-doors scrapes from Apache country to Inuit country. Great Grand was my mentor for my entry into the Bear Clan, so he thought all of this was pretty darn neat. He gave me the whole lowdown on bears and bear medicine.

Our Bear Clan has varied responsibilities. On the tribal level, our clan is entrusted with keeping order and protecting the old ways. On the healing level, we are the keepers of herbal medicine. On the spirit level, we are the protectors of Mother Earth. Those responsibilities represent Bear Power, Bear Knowledge, and Bear Vision. Great Grand said that it was my Spirit Bear that repre-sented all these things and had come in the past to teach the Ojibwe people.

Great Grand said it was the Spirit Bear who taught us the proper way to hunt, to cleanse one's body and spirit, to make an offering to Mother Earth of tobacco, and to give heartfelt thanks to that which feeds you. He said it was the Spirit Bear that taught us that you must approach hunting and fishing prayerfully, never demanding, but requesting that the creature see fit to give its life to sustain your family's. This is the lesson of respect and balance, not the outlook of trophies and dominance.

At 12, I was out on the lake alone, a lost boy in a canoe in the mist. The Spirit Bear guided me back to Bad River, swimming ahead of me. After that Great Grand picked up the pace of my lessons. "Never take a nap in a bear's den," he said, "or you'll sleep through the whole winter." Or he would point out our relationship to bears, like "The bears are our closest relatives, they will often guide lost

Anishinabe children back home."

He felt very strongly about the place of the bear in spirit teachings. He was convinced that the Spirit Bear controls the seasons in the Lake Superior area. He told me that the Spirit Bear would sometimes poke out his head from the winter den and scold the cold away, growling at the snow spirits with hot breath. And it was said that everywhere he ambled on his spring walks was opened to the return of the green spirits which breath life into the plant brothers. Then he talked of the place the Spirit Bear occupies in the sacred sweat lodge. There those who are tied to bear medicine sit in the North during the ceremonies. The north is a powerful location in things of the spirit and there is a reason that bears are associated with that location. It is the place of deep contemplation and the symbolic death of winter, for bears are reborn every spring.

Once I understood these lessons and let the Spirit Bear into my heart, then it could show up almost anywhere that I was hunting or fishing. It's an unusual bear since it loves water and these in-between places. It has shown itself to me everywhere from out on the Long Island and Chequamegon Point, over east to Marble Point, and down to Copper Falls. In each place it had something to teach me.

Now I'm in the phase of life when I teach others. It is part of the cycle of giving back as you have been given. You must give back if you want balance in the world. And you must be open to the possibility of change, open to the possibility that a big shift is coming. The Spirit Bear tells me we might be on the brink of those possibilities. I know that from how he shows himself to me now. It's no longer a matter of a young man seeing him while learning the ways of the creatures of this world. Now it's a matter of him revealing himself when the health of Mother Earth is in danger. Spirit Bear was down at the railroad tracks when we blocked the train carrying the toxic chemicals. Spirit Bear helped us find the poisons that were leaching into the water.

We live in a time of great change. Spirit Bear is not only a personal sign that we are in transition. But I think Spirit Bear is a sign that we are in the time of the Seventh Generation, the time when all people come to recognize the need to protect Mother Earth. Books don't do it all, nor do speeches. Some people need to have spirit move in their hearts. That's why we're lucky here on Chequamegon Bay to have the Spirit Bear.

Fourteen Mile Point's Ankou

I t's hard to hug the coast in some parts of Michigan's Upper Peninsula. That's a good thing from an environmental protection perspective, but tough on a collector of stories who depends on the cadence of those steeped in the feel of a place. The initial stretch of Michigan's Lake Superior shoreline seemed to offer a bounty of potential tales. Friends of friends sent me looking in the Porcupine Mountain Wilderness for tales of macabre death along the region's watery edge. There were tantalizing hints of lakefarer homicides, shipwrecks, and epidemic-stricken "Lost Dutchmen." Alas, none among the living saw fit to disclose further details to me.

Up the coast I found more leads, sketchy, but worthy of pursuit. Supposedly there was once a haunting by a ghostly fisherman in the environs of the town of Ontonagon and an auxiliary tale of a boat forever adrift. It was also suggested that there were those on the Ontonagon Reservation who told about the lingering spirit of a European American whose affair of the heart with a local American Indian young lady came to a bad end. Even these more solid story lines came to naught in my investigation.

But, as sometimes happens in this vocation, digging for one thing leads to the uncovering of another. Flustered after shuttling back and forth between the town and the reservation, I felt as if there was an aridity of narrative twixt Wisconsin and the Keweenaw Peninsula. So I sat and sputtered in the only place open that would sell me an Old Style beer. Sorcey was one of those kindly old gentlemen who hated to see anyone go through a hard time. So he asked me the source of my discomfort and offered up this consolation prize.

*   *   *

We've got rumors about ghosts all over the area. But I never meet anyone who has actually seen a ghost here in town. Which makes us odd, I guess, with the number of over-imbibers we have locally. You'd think somewhere one of their pink elephants would take on a ghostly hue.

Now out on the water it's a different matter. Out there we have a strange breed of spirit creature. Something that seems out of place and not consistent with its own kind. We have an ankou. I can tell by the look on your face that the term doesn't ring a bell. Well it's a pretty obscure thing and there are only two places in the world where ankous operate as far as I know. The region of Brittany in France was once thick with them. Then there's our solitary ankou, the one called the Fourteen Mile Point's Ankou.

It was my maternal grandmother who told me about the ankou, at least what it did around here. I learned more about it over time. We always knew there was a French link, but little beyond that. Everybody I know is a mish-mash of bloodlines up here and hardly anybody knows much about their family further back than about three generations. But this is a real old story, or at least the roots are old.

I was at a music festival in Marquette about ten years ago and heard a quartet that did what they called French celtic music. I always thought celtic meant Irish, but I learned celtic could mean just about anyplace in old Europe not pillaged and ravished by Germans and Slavs. This little band had a song about an ankou in Brittany, a sad mournful ballad.

After that I made a point of looking into the history of the ankou in Brittany and found it was rich and generally land-bound. In Brittany the ankou is associated with the oldest settlements. In fact, it seems like it's a matter of municipal pride to have a localized ankou legend. The more developed areas of commerce and housing are deemed lacking in character and unworthy of an ankou. In olden times each parish was supposed to have its own individual ankou. And they each had distinct personalities. One might have a little sense of humor and another might tarry at a wine cellar.

But in Brittany the ankou also has some standard characteristics that make it a spirit of terra firma. First off, it has an annual cycle. The spirit inhabiting the ankou changes every year and is someone local. It is commonly thought the soul of the last person in a community to die in a given year comes to serve time as the ankou the following year. And it is considered bad luck to know this person who died last because as an ankou they will look for familiar targets for soul gathering.

In Brittany the ankou is the symbolic king of the dead. He collects souls and moves them along to their next stop. He is kin to the Irish banshee and has some of the same wailing tendencies. He usually appears as a tall, gaunt figure, with long hair, a beard, and raggedy robe. He's not above knocking on doors and calling out names. And in Brittany he hauls off the souls in a two-wheeled pushcart.

Now here in the U.P. it's quite a bit different. Our one ankou is usually seen in the black robes of the long ago French missionaries. Often he's stooped, some even say hunchbacked. No banshee wail for him mind you. No, more of a growl or a snarl. No knocks on the door either. Our ankou is more of a stalker, more likely to lurk about in some bushes. Heck, I knew some old-timers years ago who wouldn't allow shrubs near the house for that reason, one who kept the brush back a good hundred yards on all sides. Plus, our Fourteen Mile Point Ankou has two methods of movement, one related to water and one related to land.

It works like this. If our ankou comes to an isolated cabin away from the lake he will haul a soul off on a travois, which he navigates by virtue of an emaciated horse that he will lead by a rope halter. If the dwelling should be near water then the approach is of the maritime sort. At least in a modest way, as our ankou will arrive on a sailing skiff. This is not much more than a dingy with a patch of canvas to catch the breeze. What is unclear is how these two methods work in tandem. It has been observed more than once that the ankou has come by travois to a beached skiff. But is it that way all the time if he is hauling souls from out of sight of the lake? It's hard to know, and some tend to think the sorting mechanism is whether the soul in question comes from a land person or a water person.

What does this all boil down to? I guess I've always thought that anything like a grim reaper or soul gatherer suggests that the people you're dealing with cling rather stubbornly to life. Life is something to be cherished, that's for sure. But could it be that some hold on through fear of death or out of some hoarding stinginess that makes them resent their inability to haul their material possessions to the afterlife? You've known such people, individuals who lack the grace, faith, or spiritual depth to give up what the mortal life cycle demands that we must. It is to such people that our ankou is drawn.

I remember the first time I saw our ankou. Actually all I saw was the stubby little sail cutting through the fog on a little inlet where a big old house held one of the area's worst misers. This was over fifty years ago and we were still in the Great Depression. The old man shall remain unnamed, it doesn't matter much since he left no friends or family. That kind never does. Anyway, the man in question was comfortably well-off from timber money inheritances. But darned if he could see fit to help out a neighbor in distress. He was particularly unsympathetic toward those elderly whose poverty and sickness converged in deep distress. The old miser would dismiss community appeals for assistance as bailouts of the unworthy and throw in for good measure a denunciation of social security as "Roosevelt socialism." I saw the sail in the fog in the little inlet and then heard the next day that the old miser had died. No one was sorry.

That's how it usually was about those the ankou hauled away. Some crude fellows even called him the trash collector. That was somewhat of the attitude held out on the reservation, though the tribal members were not verbal about it. It was out on the reservation, where I had friends, that I learned about the tie to Fourteen Mile Point and how tribal members saw this whole deal. Apparently Fourteen Mile Point always had a history as a place where strange things can dwell and pass through the barrier to the other world. So when the ankou sailed forth it was from Fourteen Mile Point. Usually it sailed west along the shore. It was usually of no concern to tribal members. My friends said there were some who could see it and would taunt it. Some would joke about how it was a good thing that white people had a spirit guardian that would look after them.

It was out there on the reservation that I learned how you act around such things. You just don't want to call attention to yourself, just like you don't want an aggressive dog to see your fear. So you can look upon the Fourteen Mile Point Ankou. You just don't want him to catch you looking. If you're caught he'll give you a look that will fix a mark on you. Sometimes I think about that because a couple of years ago he kind of half-way caught me looking. I wasn't sure, maybe he wasn't sure. But I can look you in the eye and tell you that it doesn't matter. If he comes, he comes. I've had a good life. I'm ready.

Spirits of Baraga

Up in Copper Harbor local residents told me the real center of Upper Peninsula lore was to be found in Baraga. It was a tip that came with caveats, warnings, and disclaimers. Some seemed to feel that U.P. residents with an affinity for the supernatural and paranormal were drawn to Baraga, like some black-hole with the irresistible force to pull eccentrics, the spiritually inclined, and those possessed of perceptual gifts into its tight little web. Others believed Baraga had a culture of deep secrets that boiled like a cauldron and that strange as things might appear on the surface, the meatier chunks were down deep in the pot.

Armed with some contacts, I negotiated my way through a thicket of suspicious Baraga residents who were far too introverted and far too nonverbal to be of help in story collection. They left me with the old game of twenty questions and often failed to fairly tally at that. Eventually the cumulative intelligence gleaned from grunts, shrugs, and nods guided me to a long-closed service station on the outskirts of Baraga on U.S. Highway 41.

A faded sign for a gasoline brand still swung in the wind that Keweenaw Bay offered the town. The gas pumps were long gone, though the oil-stained concrete island stood in the loose gravel in remembrance of the pumps. A two-bay garage of crumbling cinder block with a tiny office area was also sentinel to another era. Rusted DeSotos and Hudsons stood as reminder of a lost automotive past. Altogether it was a scene that would not make sense to those who did not remember what came before the current roadside convenience stores.

Here one of sufficient age could nearly feel the ghosts of mid-twentieth century America. All the better was the scene behind the garage, one shielded from highway view by a high board fence. There sat rotting fishing boats like crumbling tombs on a distant shore. There rambled a series of spliced mobile homes, silvery airstream trailers, military conex storage containers, and rumpled semi-trailers like some temple complex dedicated to unknown manufacturing gods no long worshipped. There sat Briggs, nursing the leg stumps resulting from his diabetes, chewing almost an entire pouch of Red Man tobacco at once, and just bursting at the seams to tell all he knows about things strange in Baraga.

* * *

Weird! You want weird? Hell, we got weird by the ton around here, so I can sell it to you wholesale. Hell's bells, I barely know where to start or whether to fart and go blind. As long as there's been a Baraga we've had a talent for such things. I'd say it was the original Catholic father here who put us in that way, a dabbling in dark things that he pushed the "on" switch for and never found the "off" switch. You might get argument from some who feel it goes back further than that. Could be!

Where to start? Mercy, Peter at the Gate and me a locksmith! We got your everyday ghosts in town from the usual brawls, accidents, and untimely demises that we've got a franchise on. Hardly any of them stand out as anything special, 'cept maybe for some suicide related ones from a ways back. I'll skip the details since I just had lunch.

It's the general area, Baraga County and beyond, that's got the real interesting and rare stuff. It could be the minerals in the ground up here, or the waters of the lake, or how they interact. You know, like a wet cell battery. That's how it often works around here, these odd beings and queer happenings are half about the lake and half about the land.

Out toward the Huron Mountains to the east we have something that follows that pattern. They're called tree ghosts and spirit trees. Now on the surface this just seems like trees that make strange sounds. There's pockets of those throughout the U.P. I've heard of them up toward Houghton and out on Point Abbaye. But it's on the north side of the Huron Mountains where it gets a little different. There they seem to talk to each other. Yup, I've heard it, kind of a whispering in another language. Wait, it gets odder. On the slope down to the lake the trees will kind of sing. If there's loss of life out on the lake then they'll wail. I haven't heard that myself, but I have it on good authority from a man as honest as a fat man in a pickle barrel.

Out in our wrap-around L'Anse Reservation we got the Dzibai problem. Sounds like a Finnish dirty word, but it's pure Indian. Question is whether they're to blame for it or not. Some out there say that outside interference threw something out of whack. But you have some Indian-haters who claim there was a dabbling in black magic. It use to be that the Dzibai was a special ceremony to speed along a soul to its destination. So you kind of had a wake where such things were done according to custom. Supposedly someone got the bright idea that such travel assistance might just work on those still among the living. The theory was tested out a little too often and now they've got spots of lake shore where you don't want to step. Or, like the kids say, you'll get beamed up to somewhere.

Then right along this stretch of highway we've got a ghost as simple-minded as a lumberjack blowing his money on cards in a cathouse. Just up the road is what use to be a cafe. The old spirit fellow keeps coming for breakfast and looks surprised when there's no service. Truth be told, it was a place that was slow in that department even in its prime. He's likely one of the fishermen who waited for early morning service before going out in the boats.

Up a ways the shoreline we got what we call a screaming pit. It's a hole in the ground where there has been a history of hollering coming out of it. I've heard the dang thing, but it also is hard to figure it out since the screaming always stops as soon as you get to the edge and look down. So when you look down the hole there's nothing to see. There are theories about the origin of this thing, but nothing solid. One old geezer said it was a body disposal site after some epidemic. Yet there is a whiff of a rumor that a lake tragedy claimed some unconnected immigrants and that for convenience sake their bodies were thrown into the pit. I tend to think both things might have happened and perhaps another tragedy, too, since they come in threes around here. Whatever the combination, my gut detects some influence of Old Lake Superior.

This deal with the pit may relate to another weird thing that happens up and down the shore. That's the thing I call the Baraga Screaming Skull. It's just what it sounds like, a white bonehead with his yap wide open and splitting the ears of passersby. It's rare to sight the thing, but it has been seen a time or two by people I know to have eagle eye and sober brains. This jolly roger is said to be luminous at night and free-floating in the air above the shoreline. The tale involved connects to a lakefarer of British origin and in that island nation screaming skulls are said to run in families or infect those connected to certain manors. So the only question for me is whether the skull originated here through a mortal incident or was brought in a sailor's trunk. The question remains as to whether this dead noggin is a sign or omen. But when it comes to

most of these blasted boogers, I think they're just shameless atten-
tion-getters. You know their type among the living. Though there
is a school of thought that screaming skulls come from claustro-
phobes who can't stand burial.

We got tree stump ghosts, too, mostly close to the shoreline. Big
old stumps hollowed out in the center where occasional spray and
scud from the lake can fill the hole like a little wishing well. The
way these work is that you can see the faces of spirits down in that
water. Supposedly the expression on the face is kind of a fortune
telling for the one that sees it. All I've ever seen is a sleeping face.
Hope that means that I'll go easy when my time comes. One old
bugger I know said he saw a face with a stupid expression on it. I
laughed, but didn't have the heart to tell him that was because he
was the type who would use a golden net to catch suckers in a sewer.
These stump critters are probably of Indian origin, but nobody on
L'Anse will tell me a thing about them.

Finally, we got a whole barge load of irksome little spirits. Some
of them are "little people" that the L'Anse say come up out of the
lake. Another breed are called Knockers, like the English mining
ghosts. But these spritely spirits make a to-do by banging rocks
together along the shore and leaving them in circles in the sand.
They're a happy lot, like farmers working forty-acres of hops in
heaven. The other breed like that, the kobolds, is just the opposite.
They're sour and malicious. They're supposed to be shanghaied
German spirits brought here against their will. If you got a cut line
on a boat, a suspicious leak, or motor that's gummed up, they're the
likely culprits.

There's others up here, too. I could go on and on. None that are
a big problem requiring priestly intervention. I think we even got
some squeezed out of other places. I believe that Baraga is just
more tolerant about such things, more willing to look the other way
like we do for our neighbors.

Bells of Whitefish Point

Reaction to a drive along the north side of the Upper Peninsula can vary with the dispositions of those traversing its forest roads. Those focused on destinations and human activities often find the highway stretches boring and lonely. On the other hand those attuned to nature can find delights, large and small, in the expanses that are easily accessible. Some say that they are too readily accessible and that the eastern U.P., in particular, is being loved to death.

My own trips in those environs confirm the anomaly of it being a place where one can often be out of sight of human eyesores and nevertheless almost never be out of earshot of human discord. Perhaps it is decibel level that accounts for my story-collecting woes in this particular regions. Many a lead thereabouts put me in proximity to potential sources who could barely be constrained to shut off chainsaws, snowmobiles, and ATVs or who were loathe to cease and desist target shooting. My own fondness for the exuberant life and tavern sociability notwithstanding, I usually find that both the teller of and the listener to a good story benefit from a brief interlude of preceding silence. Here I often found loud and friendly people whose conversation repertoire consists of "huh", "what did you say?" and "I can't hear you."

Experience dictated that I either retreat deeper into the forests or seek out more reflective folk. Whilst story-collecting it is precisely that impulse that sends me into those spots where whispers are more common than beer-chugging hoots. That's how I come to find myself in archives, old churches, and museums.

Sometimes I just drive. When things aren't proceeding as I had hoped I will drive away from those conditions. But it is inevitable that the trip away will bring you to something. In this case it was a U.P. town called Paradise, a name with a rather boastful charm. There I picked up Farrell, the oldest hitchhiker who has ever climbed in my truck. He showed me some sights I might have missed and told me a story that had my ears ringing in a different way.

*   *   *

Going toward Whitefish Point? Well, I'll go all the way or as far as you're going. I'm from up that way originally. Not much up there anymore. Not much anywhere in the U.P. that I can see, unless you've latched onto tourist or paper company tit. Suck them for what they're worth if you must, but never think that they'll love you back. They'll drop you as soon as it suits them.

You going up to see the museum? What museum? Holy sleigh bells, the Great Lakes Shipwreck Museum, that's what museum. Don't get all cranked up and rupture yourself. I just meant to tell you that the museum probably isn't open right now. If you're around for a couple of days you should visit it. I thought you might be headed to Whitefish Point to see it. A honest man must confess that there isn't much else in Whitefish Point to see.

If you drive me all the way up there I can help you peek around the museum. There's things you can see from the outside. Who knows, there might be someone to let us in or we might find things unlatched. Never let technicalities interfere with your education, I say.

Now I could tell you the whole history of Whitefish Point, but I'd rather you stay awake on the drive there. It's just the usual Genesis story of who beget who, who was struck down by the Almighty's fury, who got flooded, was turned into a pillar of salt, or got loaded on hooch and babbled like at the Tower of Babel. And you don't know anybody there, right? So for you it would just be Joe Blow, Mary Blow, their little baby Hey-Zeus Blow, all the other low blows, and who you know and who you blow.

As for stories, Noah in a rowboat, we got stories. Ghosts though, not much there except the usual creaking floors and late night funny business. But when it come to weird, we got weird. We had a fellow that had nose hair so long he could braid it. We had a crazy gal who made art out of tampons. And strange lights, like much of the U.P., we got strange light flying right out of the Almighty's rectum.

Still, the thing that tingles my jingle and jangles my dangle is the bells. You never heard of the bells? I happen to think the bells are our oldest story and a story that keeps growing over time. At least I've heard stories of the bells that have their roots all the way back to 1861.

That's when the old red-roof light station was built to save shipping. Our shoreline was already known at that point as "shipwreck coast." A name it continued to earn for some time. Supposedly the light station site was picked not only for geography and navigation sake, but because people heard bells at the point. Yes, they heard bells that couldn't be linked to any particular source.

Sure, there was talk about an old French mission and its bells, but I never saw a shred of real evidence for that claim. There's no ruin and no record of such a religious structure or anything like it. The ship bells theory held a little more water. This was the idea that one or more vessels in distress sent their final sounds out by bell clanging in the moments below they slipped beneath old Lake Superior's cold gray water. I heard the dang thing years ago and it was a light bell, like a brass bell on a sailboat. But others heard it as a big iron one as you might hear on an old steamer. A few even hear it as a naval ship bell. It must be heard as what people expect. Our main fishing guide hears it as a cow bell.

How the bells work is a confusing issue. You'd almost think they'd be solely a harbinger of disaster. But it seems to have several ways of operating. It's true that bells were heard several times and followed by reports of ships sinking. It's also happened that folks in light craft have been caught in waves too large for their liking only to hear the bells and have the water go calm like the story of the Sea of Galilee. Others have heard the bells as signal for round one for a fifteen round bout with heavyweight champion Superior and the beginning of woes as varied as Jonah's, Lazurus's, and Lot's put together.

There could be lots of reasons why this happens around White-fish Point. It's probably because of our place in the world and our place on the lakes. It's the turning point for upbound ships. For newcomers in autumn this is where they get a dose of Lake Superior reality. But it's a turning point in other ways, symbolic and feeling-wise, that are a little harder to explain. There's a shift in lake mood when you round Whitefish Point. I've felt it. There's just a little something more direct about the power of Lake Superior to the west of the point.

I've found others up here along the lake who experienced the same thing. Especially if they're of an age to have hauled nets and worked the lines in the old way. I've heard that feeling expressed about Whitefish Point over by Point Iroquois Light Station and at Bay Mills Indian reservation. I've had a nod or two when I've mentioned the bells to folks in those places, especially at Point Iroquois. You know, there's a museum over there, too. One old boy at the museum told me that this stuff with the bells is related to the wrecks and the collected ship artifacts of the area.

This would make sense in a way, especially after the loss of the *Edmund Fitzgerald*. You know that the big ore ship went down seventeen miles northwest of Whitefish Point in that awful November of 1975, don't you? So that crew of twenty-nine is in the deep watery tomb out there. More to the point, guess what's up at that Great Lakes Shipwreck Museum? Well let me tell you, they got the bell of the Edmund Fitzgerald. Ain't that a hell of a note?

Now I told you that this wasn't exactly a ghost story. But I'll throw in a teaser for free. Shortly after they got the Fitzgerald's bell up there was an incident about a late night ringing of the darn thing. That was never explained. Nor was it ever explained why a lakeman named McSorley kept asking for directions to the museum at odd hours. You probably don't know it, but Captain McSorley was the master of the Edmund Fitzgerald.

Be that as it may, the bells keep ringing. I'll bet they'll keep ringing until Gabriel sounds his trumpet and the riders of death bring the end-time. Then this old lake will give up its dead. Ding, dong, we'll all be gone.

Part VI
Down Lake Passage
on Michigan

Manistique's Swimming Moose

After rounding the north coast Upper Peninsula I had hoped to fall back on more familiar sources and reliable leads. Back in the late 1980s, work in environmental coalitions found me traveling Lake Michigan's northwest coast several times a year. During that time I heard about a baker's dozen hints of odd happenings between Mackinac and Green Bay sufficiently intriguing to jot down as reminders for subsequent investigation.

We humans often make assumptions about availability, continuity, and even mortality that do not hold up under life's unpredictable circumstances. The dutiful notation of potential sources and the filing away of same for a decade or more is such a gamble with fate. This was the story collector's lesson in actuarial realities: Interview your oldest sources first. The baker's dozen on the stretch of coast dwindled down to a convenience store four-pack by the time I actually tackled this collection in earnest. Most of the white-hairs of my notes had faded from this earth.

This leaves me with no story thread about the ghostly woman sailor of Gros Cap. No one living could give credence to the lead about a floating coffin once seen off Point Patterson. No tale of the phantom 17th Century French ship is still told at Fairport. None living in Escanaba still laugh at the improbable but delightful notion of inebriated Scandinavians recreating a Viking funeral by setting a wooden rail boxcar on a raft afire, only to be haunted by cremated decedent. Those and many other story remnants in these parts disappeared under the waves to await investigations with greater marine archeology skills than my own.

Still, the story collecting travails involved in finding survivors in the area brought me fresh material as well. Fresh contacts often see with fresh eyes. In Manistique I found an old source's dwelling inhabited by a relative newcomer. As I found with "Mather's Shaman" (Northern Frights) in Wisconsin, some of those moving into our region bring different forms of spiritual attunement to the task of interpreting paranormal phenomena. In Jan's kitchen, with its view of Lake Michigan, I found someone far more attuned to the Earth's creatures than anyone I had ever met before.

* * *

Animals are constantly trying to tell us things and we hardly ever listen. That's why I moved up the coast from Menominee. I had to get somewhere with more direct contact with animals, more space, and more quiet. You must still the mind and sharpen the senses if you want to see such things.

If you find the spot that calls to you, well, you can then hear the messages of all its living beings and the echoes of those that came before. I grew up a city girl, went to school in Green Bay and Chicago, and the idea of being in relationship with animals would have been strange to me twenty years ago. But after college I went to Ireland to explore family roots and quite accidently fell into some lessons in old Celtic magic about animals. So since then I've studied almost all the old nature-based cosmologies on all the inhabited continents. I've learned from Lapps, Hopis, Mayans, and Wiccans. I've also learned from volunteering to rehabilitate injured animals.

People around here think I'm a bit odd because of this outlook, especially when I share what I've seen and heard. Partly, it's the way that people relate to a woman who lives alone by choice, especially one who kayaks the lake from Seul Choix to Aux Barques. Partly, it's because they think that this is the site of lesbian orgies and bestiality. About as wild as it gets here is when a few friends show up with fiddles and guitars.

I guess I should have never told anyone about the moose. I just assumed that others had seen it. Usually, even with a magical or spirit animal, others will see it if it's a manifestation of the life force of a particular area. My swimming moose is certainly that, almost as strong an entity as one would encounter.

Moose are around in the U.P., though not abundant. They will occasionally wander close to the town. So it's not as if the idea of a moose-sighting is outrageous. It's more the fact that I usually see it out in Lake Michigan and no one else does. Guess they're just not ready to see it.

The first time I saw it was my first moonlight kayak jaunt on the lake. It surfaced directly in front of me and the moonlight made his wet antlers glisten. It stared directly at me and I have never felt as strong a telepathic connection with any creature, human or animal. It overwhelmed me emotionally to the point of tears. When my eyes cleared it was gone. So began my learning about the moose. I can share most of it.

When the moose comes into your life you are in contact with the most basic feminine energy, even if the moose is male. It's a land animal that is a powerful water sign. It was a powerful confirmation that I had come to the right place.

To see a moose in deep water is an even more powerful sign. It is further sign of deep connection to the liquid elements that sustain life, bring forth life, and sustain creativity. I've learned that to see one under the circumstances I first did is to be sent a message that you are in the presence of the elemental forces of life and death.

An American Indian on a pilgrimage across North America told me what he had learned about the magical significance of moose. He told me that in Nova Scotia the Micmac say that the moose was once a whale and if hunted too often it returns to the sea. Maybe that has some bearing on the way my moose appears to me. He also said that moose are strong symbols in late fall and early winter, symbols of approaching shadow.

The second time I saw the moose out in the lake it was through the spotting scope I use to birdwatch. It was just getting light, with a light gray mist sitting on calm water like meringue. He was coming out of the water, dripping lake water in small rivulets. What a contradiction, I thought, so ungainly looking and yet graceful in a powerful way. The strength is as obvious as the size, yet there are the traits of stealth and camouflage. This ability to freeze and blend into the landscape is what makes the moose the special animal of shapeshifters and magicians. Just to see a moose is a sign that you are *allowed* to see it.

This relationship with Manistique's swimming moose is what evolved into my understanding of the moose as my animal totem. In that capacity it becomes teacher, confidant, agent of dreams, protector, and guide on my journey through Nature. A moose totem is very powerful. It is extremely useful for contacting all manner of spirits and for traveling to the places of the dead.

Keen senses in the moose make it very unusual for a large mammal. When I have encounters with this one there is obvious intelligence in its aura. The huge antlers give it direct connection to the upper chakhras. The overall energy is one of strong sexuality and celebration of the creation of life and of birthing.

This duality in the moose is interesting, this interweaving of life and death themes. The third time I saw the moose was on a beach walk on October 31st, Halloween, All-Souls' eve, or, as the old celtic observers of Nature called it, Samhain. At such times it is a significant connection to those who have crossed over to the other side. When I came back from that walk all manner of spirits made their presences known. My candles flickered as if there was a breeze in the house. The cupboards rattled and the pantry floor creaked. I left Irish whiskey in a glass and it was gone in the morning.

The moose is also a teacher of herbal medicine. There is a strong connection to the plant world through the moose. He is, after all, just about the biggest herbivore in this hemisphere. This one helped me locate some aquatic plants that have special properties. I needed something and was at a loss for a remedy. Then the moose appeared and I followed him in a marsh-fed estuary. He went under and came up with a plant I have never seen before. I knew it had to be a sign, so I gathered some and used it. I was very impressed with the results.

So you probably think I'm crazy after I've told you all this. Look me in the eye, listen to my voice, and take my hand. I can't tell you if this is a mortal animal or a mystical creature. But I can tell you that it has the ability to alter human life. It sure has altered mine.

Log Jockeys of Escanaba

*N*o matter what the line of inquiry in Escanaba, the story line usually comes back to things involving timber. No matter that the
questions revolve around railroading, mining, the Cedar River
*Potawatomi, the big bucks of Hiawatha National Forest, or the secret fish-
ing spots of Big Bay de Noc, the narrative will always come back to the
trees, the saw logs, and the men who moved them. That was the case when
I probed several generations of Upper Peninsula railroading in "Ties that
Bind"* (Prairie Whistles: Tales of Midwest Railroading). *It was still
the case when I sniffed about Escanaba for hints of things spooky or weird.*

The first rumor that I chased was one about "floaters," phantoms of unfortunate workers who took fatal tumbles off the ore docks.
The story still had currency at the end of the 20th Century, but I
couldn't find anyone who had actually seen these apparitions of
industrial accidents. Instead there was an "official" explanation
that these "floaters" were the man-sized chucks of wood refuse from
the Chicago and North Western railroad's tie plant that sometimes
bobbed along Escanaba's waterfront.

*In the course of that goose chase I did hear quite a bit of timber lore.
Some of it had a lake connection back to sailing packet ships after the Civil
War. Some of it could be traced to the rugged breed of men who bucked up
firewood on Lake Michigan's islands in order to sell it as fuel for passing
steamboats. It was in those tavern and cafe gabfests in Escanaba that I
met Gabe and heard him tally the toll of logging on body and soul. In his
view this toll is ongoing.*

*   *   *

Every human endeavor of any magnitude leaves spirits behind
it its wake. These ghostly log jockeys are part of that tradition.
There was a physical cost to logging industry work that made these
spirit reverberations inevitable. This situation is a bit different because it involved the lake tool.

Now I'm not saying that those who worked logs on rivers didn't
have their hazards too. Sometimes a spring log run after the thaw
was almost like whitewater navigation, shooting rapids and small

falls. Plus those river timber pilots had the dangers of the jams and pileups that had to be blasted apart with explosives. Many in that line of work bought the farm, as they say. But, like as not, their bodies ended up in the bays and mill harbors where the logs ended up after the run.

There were many names for the work of sorting, mustering, and moving the logs on a big body of water. I've heard them called timber herders, peavey men, the wooden cavalry, sawlog cowboys, and, of course, log jockeys. They did several types of work involving sorting, grading, chaining, lashing, pushing logs, and building booms. Most people don't realize it, but it was common to have the logs of more than one company end up in the same body of water, sort of like cattle on the open range. Just like cattle can have a brand, logs were sometimes stamped on the butt end. It's easy to guess that working acres of slippery logs on the lake might lead to a casualty now and then.

What made log jockeying on the lake hard was the sheer volume of logs and the fact that they were not easily confined to the sawmill harbors. Big lakes, including this one, have fickle weather, with currents and winds that make for challenges. Like their counterparts on the rivers, the lake log jockeys could easily slip and take a header into the drink. On the rivers this meant getting your head busted by the swift moving logs. On the lake it was usually more a matter of not being able to find the space to get back up for air. It was almost like being swallowed up by a crevice on a glacier. One minute a log jockey could be nimbly picking his way across the mass of logs, the next minute he would be gone without a trace.

This leads some people to see the reflections of these men's faces in the depths of the water. They usually have a surprised look on their faces, eyes wide with the desperate last struggle for air. I've seen such faces down about five to ten feet in Little Bay de Noc. And no, these are not the ore dock floaters. Those are a different breed of haunting, rarer I'd say. Besides, those floaters usually have a banged up look since they were often dead before they hit the water.

There's another type of log jockey ghost that I know of as well. These fellows are the lost timber herders. These are the ones said to have been working the booms and wide logfields that went adrift on the lake. You know how it is with weather that can shift suddenly. Well, I guess some log jockeys were working patches of floating logs that became detached from the main log field and then

blew out into the lake. It's not like the log outfits didn't try to retrieve these men, but every once in awhile they would find a patch
of sawlogs in the middle of the lake with no log jockey in sight.
These fellows are said to still call out for help out on the lake. I've
thought I've heard them a time or two, but it's very faint.

I've also heard about another manifestation of the swept away
log jockey. These are the ones who were caught out on the lake
when those unexpected freezing storms came up and blew logs and
men adrift. Usually there were immediate rescue efforts to retrieve
them. The problem was usually the temperature. A man cannot
survive for long on logs in pitching waves, freezing rain, snow, or
subzero windchills.

Sometimes such men were found frozen to the logs, coated with
a glaze of ice that made them look like porcelain mannequins. Sometimes the ghosts of such men are still seen clinging to logs in cold
choppy water. Maybe the mind plays tricks, but I've had a half
dozen times when I've been out in the lake and thought I've seen
such things. It's never a matter of a false impression, like a tree
with a thick limb or a cracked up crate. No, when I investigate and
move closer it always turns out that there's nothing there at all.

That's the thing about these log jockey ghosts, they're not optical illusions or matters of mistaken identification. Many so-called
ghost sightings are just objects seen in peculiar ways because of light-
ing, angle, or the powers of suggestion. These log jockeys are horses
of a different color. They're there and then they're not. They don't
leave so much as a trace behind. There's rarely so much as a ripple
where they were seen.

These Great Lakes are so big, there's so much room for mystery
and strange things in them. Who knows what lurks in Little Bay de
Noc from the logging, mining, and rail days? Who knows what
ancient things from the Potawatomi and other old peoples lie at the
bottom Big Bay de Noc? Why would we think that such things
would come and go and not leave a ripple in the film of ether that
separates the seen and unseen worlds?

You also need to think about the people who did this work of
moving logs on water and paid the price for the dangers. Mostly
Scandinavians, Norwegians, and Finns, through the big years of
the timber boom. Many of them had worked logs on fjords and
wild rivers in the old countries. So the possibility of great bodily
harm and death was not unknown to them. They also knew the
claim that cold waters have on the bodies of warm-blooded men.

Lastly, they knew the pull of the spirits that were already in the big bodies of water. They knew that those already there were eager to be joined by more.

Had things gone on as in the peak years there might have been a steady supply of log jockeys joining them in the bays. But the industry changed, sputtered, and then pretty much died off. The big spring log runs only lasted a few decades at most. Moving the logs on the bays took on a different look when steam tugs started assisting the pushing to mills. After that they rafted them and shoved them like barges. The railroads got up here and worked the woods away from the rivers.

This last development was responsible for the weirdest log jockey ghost story I ever heard. They started making railroad ties in Escanaba after all the really big timber was gone. Most of those got shipped out by rail, but some were loaded on ships to save the trip around the lake by rail. I heard that one ship loaded stacks of ties on its deck and that they were swept off in a storm. This accounts for the odd occasional sightings of a ghostly log jockey working a jam of ties far out in the lake. He's been seen nimbly hopping the big bobbing switch ties and vaulting with his peavey as the lake swells lifted and dropped these barn beam size chunks of lumber.

I've never seen that one. Only a few have. But I'm keeping an eye out for him.

Old Hag's Boat

The roads leading me back to Wisconsin from Escanaba were lined with curios and characters that merit preservation in print. But the problem previously mentioned concerning the attrition of sources on the supernatural held true through the remainder of my Upper Peninsula sojourn. There were no shortages of sources on memorable storms, maritime mishaps, and unforgettable characters tied to the lakes. Unfortunately, there was little that related to hauntings, curses, strange creatures, or other paranormal experiences.

A few clues brought me to a marina in Menominee, Michigan, in pursuit of an alleged lake monster. Reports made it sound like a Great Lakes version of Scotland's Loch Ness creature. Dockside versions were cryptic and more dismissive: "That was long ago," "Haven't heard that story in years," "Feller drinks enough in a boat in the full sun, he's likely to see anything," and the more crude and boastful "That was just me taking a leak."

Stuff like that is good for a few chuckles, but it's hard on the serious collector of supernatural lore, especially if one's intent is to fill in a regional slot in a larger string of stories. It's the type of initial response that often leads to a decision to put the project aside and start afresh another day. Being inclined by nature to the "if you can't beat them, then join them" school of thought and action, I found myself plunked on said marina dock with six or seven residents of the Menominee, Michigan, and Marinette, Wisconsin, areas. Liberal contributions to their revolving fund for the endowment of continuous Miller High Life resupply brought me into this crusty circle and made its members more forthcoming in their revelations. Lubricated openness notwithstanding, the monster reference still came to naught.

Story payoff came in a different form, courtesy of my familiarity with malt beverages, bulk of body, and devotion to the narrative cause (the rumors about two hollow legs are not true). The more profane of those assembled faded away one by one until I was left alone with Keith, a seasonally employed construction worker who cheerfully awaited layoffs that facilitated outdoor recreation and beer drinking. Though just entering his thirtieth summer, he was as thoughtful a blue-collar worker as I had met in a long time. We sat quietly on the dock, and for a time the only sound was the lapping of the water. He broke the silence with an admission that deserves re-telling.

* * *

I don't know anything about lake monsters, but I can tell you something strange that's been bothering the hell out of me. It's part dream and part things I see during the day. Buy the more I think about it the less sure I am about which is which. Hell, how do we know what's real and what's a dream?

It all started for me one day out on the lake when I thought I saw a strange boat, if a boat is what you'd call such a contraption. At first I thought maybe a lake side cabin or drawbridge shack had slid into the lake and was floating around out there. 'Cause that is what it looked like sitting about a mile or two away, some part of building floating out there.

Naturally I wanted to get closer for a look, so I steered for it and pushed the throttle. I made up a little of the gap and could see that it was bigger than I thought and configured different than I thought. It was probably further away than I first thought since I could now see that it was a two story structure sitting on a boat hull. It was as strange a thing as I've seen afloat, multicolored salvage and flapping rags. If I had to describe it I'd say it looked like the result of a collision between a yacht, a barn with a faded chewing tobacco sign, and old motor home, and several miles of used car lot banners. How it would float was my biggest question at the time.

So I tried to answer that question. But as I got closer it seemed to make evasive maneuvers. First zigzagging and then picking up speed and disappearing over the horizon. How it did that is a mystery, but it was doing better than thirty knots in five foot waves while I was bottom-slapping. It was aimed southeast, toward Ludington. I saw no human activity on it, no sign of a bridge or pilothouse.

That night I had the strangest dream. I was in a darkened room, laying on my back on the lid of a pine coffin. It was if I was paralyzed, I tried to get up and couldn't move anything except my eyeballs. After a bit I could sense the room swaying slightly. All of a sudden I knew that I was in the boat that I had seen out on the lake. I panicked and tried to scream but I couldn't. Then I woke up.

Troubling stuff, but it faded in a few days. About a month later I saw the damn junk boat again. Hell, I even called the Coast Guard about it. They said they'd take a report, but I could tell they thought I was a mental case. Just like before, I couldn't catch up to it.

Well, what should happen that night but another dream like the first one. Only this time I'm buck naked on the coffin and an old woman comes in the room, smelling like twenty years of carp cleaning without a bath. Just like a chimp she jumps up and sits on me. Again I try to scream and can't. Then I wake up sweating and shivering. I almost went to counseling. But nothing happened again for a long while so I just put it behind me.

Next summer comes and I saw that damn houseboat from hell on the lake again. This time I got close enough to hear sounds on the damn thing. Not engine sounds, more like organ music and screaming. I got the overwhelming sense that the screams were my screams. So I opened up the gas and got out of there.

Needless to say I was dreading the next dream. I drank four or five pots of coffee that night in an effort to stay up and avoid a nightmare. But a buddy dropped in after bar time and I made the mistake of telling him the whole story. He was drunk enough that it made perfect sense to him and he offered the usual north country remedy of a bottle of cheap whiskey, which we drank in about two hours. In spite of the coffee, I was out like a candle in a urinal by dawn.

The dream hit me like a front-end loader full of rock. I was back on the boat, old lady on top of me. This time she was riding me like I was a rodeo bull. It was terrifying and yet...well, I'm not going there. Anyway I woke up and felt like I had done ten rounds with Mike Tyson and had every appendage bitten off.

That drove me to research. I went up to the university at Marquette, looked in the library, and got on the Internet. I looked at this from every angle I could. Everything from dream symbolism to abnormal psychology to mythology to psychic phenomena. That's how I learned about the tradition of the Old Hag. It seemed to grow out of an old medical diagnosis called "night terror."

This is a whole tradition of dream-state assaults with sexual overtones. It goes back to the time when morning exhaustion and restless sleep were attributed to the nighttime visit of a witch who molested the victim. Later another school of thought blamed this disorder on vampires. More modern times have brought allegations of alien abductions, microchip implants, and probes of orifices. Take it a step further and you're right on black helicopter and cattle mutilation territory.

There are some common features to this night terror tradition. There are strong sensory associations with visual symbols, irritating sounds, and obnoxious smells. There is the common thread of paralysis or immobilization. The Hag cannot be dislodged while the victim is sleeping. Also, there's always a gruesome appearance combined with a raw animal power.

It's this combination that makes the psychologist chalk up the phenomena to repressed sexuality. I don't want to get into bragging, but that is not my problem. The people who look at this from a witch angle see it as the result of a curse. But, these episodes aside, I'm a pretty happy-go-lucky guy. The alien and conspiracy stuff, well, I don't know. It seems to me that if little green men or the government wanted to mess with your head they'd get better cooperation if they made up their representatives to look like Cameron Diaz and booked a suite at the Hilton.

The boat and the dream connection don't exactly jump out at your either. I mean, if these things were going to come to you in the night you wouldn't really need a daytime optical illusion, hallucination, or bad tequila episode involving a high-speed hovel on a hull. But the boat is definitely a trigger, like a flashing light can be for a migraine. O.K. then, what is the boat, what would old Doc Freud have to say about that? The interior of the boat is as distinctive as the dream encounter.

There's an old ship's clock in that room that strikes twelve when the dream starts. There's a brass wash basin with faintly bloody water in it. There's a trumpet suspended from the ceiling that manages to blast a note when the dream is about to end. There are tall black candles that smell like licorice. Fish nets hang on the walls. And the coffin is decorated with beer bottle labels.

I did a stupid thing and asked an old girlfriend who is now a social worker what it meant. I didn't give her all the details, but she didn't even hesitate in answering. She said it represented the symbolic rape and death of the blue collar male, who, having been snared in the net of the rickety ship of industrial capitalism, was going down with the ship and seeing his youthful dreams burn up while he drank himself into a stupor. What a bunch of psychobabble!

Though she may have something there with the drinking end of it. I noticed that I always had a snootful when the dream hit me and I was always a little under the weather from a rough night when I saw the weird tub out in the lake. Then there's another alcohol connection, too, as I found out talking to two buddies. My admission of the weirdness brought confessions of similar experiences from them. We compared notes and discovered that it all started around the time one of the guys got some homemade wine from an old lady over in Marinette. He was fooling around with the old gal's granddaughter, without the benefit of honorable intentions as they say. Supposedly that wine was made with herbs and other stuff she gathered up. We knocked back a gallon of the swill one night and a couple days later we started having strange experiences.

That fits with the Old Hag stories about the night terrors being the result of spells, potions, and other magical manipulation. The old lady from Marinette fits with the legends too. Supposedly she is a former nun who got kicked out of the convent after getting pregnant. Then she went to work on fishing boats to support her kid. They say she drank whiskey, smoked a pipe, and got a gross tattoo on her ass.

I haven't seen the boat or dreamed about this stuff for awhile. But I'm ready for it now. If it comes my way again I'm going to chase that hobo yacht all the way down the St. Lawrence River. And if I have that dream again I'm not going to fight. Hell no, I'll just relax and enjoy.

Phantoms of
the Seaman's Ministry

Green Bay friends promised to line me up with a guide for a tour of Sturgeon Bay, Rock Island, and Algoma. Those spots, they assured me, were blessed with abundant lore and reports of hauntings and odd sightings. Inquiries about Green Bay itself, not to mention the marsh and river country around Peshtigo and Oconto, failed to elicit as much enthusiasm among my sources.

Fortunately their mentor in such things was far better informed. Merl knew the Wisconsin coastline from Marinette to Port Washington, having fished it and sailed it in a handmade boat. This energetic retiree caught up with me in a Green Bay hotel lobby and within ten minutes regaled me with salty tales from his twenty years in the U.S. Navy and his twenty-five years on commercial sea and lake vessels. That brief encounter was just a warm-up.

The next morning he picked me up at the dock behind my hotel. Our excursion for the day involved a trip to Long Tail Point to see the haunted ruins of the old lighthouse on that island. He promised plenty of background narrative and a few wild yarns that he'd throw in for my consideration. It seemed like a promising preliminary round for the subsequent field trips he was planning for me in Door and Kewaunee counties. He surprised me with far more material then one has a right to expect.

The trip to Long Tail Point is not long, but it was long enough for Merl to relate eight other stories related to Green Bay. It was not easy to decide which one to use in this collection. He caught my interest with a tale of ghostly openings of local drawbridges. He tugged at my train connections with a report of an eerie green glow to the swing rail bridge. He knew of evil deeds associated with the Grassy Island range lights. He entertained me with tales of drunken Coast Guardsmen gone mad at the Green Bay Harbor Entrance Light. He offered theories about the fate of one missing crewman of the long gone Peshtigo Reef Lightship. He told of suspicious fires and lightkeeper premonitions of the Great Peshtigo Fire up at the Green Island Light.

Who would have thought that I'd be reeled in by a haunted house story? This is the ghost story archetype that I find least interesting and I did not expect that many of this type would relate to the Great Lakes. Merl proved me wrong.

*   *   *

Most of what I've told you so far has to do with purely local stuff. You have to look at these things on the Great Lakes on several different levels. At the basic level you have stories connected to short run ferries, pleasure raft marinas, and things that are non-commercial. Then you have commercial fishing, cross-lake ferries, and long distance sailing. Next you have the traffic on major vessels, like the ore ships serving the down-lake mills and even the grain ships going overseas.

One of the strangest things I've ever heard that ties to the shipping end has to do with those who manned the big ships and the hardships of their lives. I'm talking about a place back in the city, a place where mariners came to rest and deal with their cares. I believe it started back in the days of the early sailing vessels and went right up to the Seaway time. It was called different things at different times, the Sailor's Home, the Seaman's Club, the Lakefarers Rest, and the Seaman's Ministry.

It was at the corner of Chestnut and Kellog in the old Fort Howard area. It was just a block west of Broadway's strip of dives, you know, over past the tracks on that side of the Fox River. It was a big old mansion, three full stories. Back in those days you could come in off a ship and catch a train back to Milwaukee or Chicago to find another ship. You could drink yourself senseless on Broadway and sleep it off in the flops, or you could keep yourself out of trouble at the Seaman's Ministry.

Almost every port city of any size had such a place and I've heard of cities where they still thrive. Such places are like USOs or enlisted men's clubs for maritime men. I've heard of a few that were haunted by solitary souls, usually old salts who were too old for another passage. The sailor's home or mission arose out of that steaming goulash of the late 1800s when political progressives and social gospel clergy were out to save all who needed saving. So such a place could be a blend of temperance society, evangelism, leftwing politics, union organizing, and just plain do-gooderism. Or it could be the outgrowth of the local elite's campaign to stamp out vice not under their control.

The one at Chestnut and Kellog streets was of more modest origins and aims, the handed down scuttlebutt claiming genesis in the hands of a congregation-less man of the cloth. Maybe that's what fed speculation on events there and later embellished yarns. The imagination has a lot to work with an itinerant preacher. Is he legitimate? What might his role be in any ensuing swindles and mayhem? Might he be a clever psychopath working a comfortable scam? Not that any man on dry land or afloat has the answers to such bunk rack speculation. All who would note the correction to that compass heading are in the ground or in the deep.

At Chestnut and Kellog streets there certainly was enough story load to fill the mental cargo holds of the phantom ships that sail through men's fearful imaginations. The Seaman's Ministry in its later days was a fertile place for the sounds of feet running on companionway steps, the clanking of anchor chain, the raging of surf, the cry of gulls, and the profane curses of men working a wave-swept deck. Then there were the late night apparitions or phantoms. Even after the home was torn down to make way for a school, those phantoms made their treks to and fro between the home and the docks. They had the look of lost and forlorn men, trudging with bundles or seabags. I know, I saw them as a boy and strange as it sounds that's part of what made me want to look around the world on ships, to see what they saw.

The claim was that there had been plenty of death on that home. I guess influenza swept through it a time or two. The locals were even of a belief that the home's occupants were the source of whatever disease scourges happened to arrive in Green Bay. As a matter of disease patterns, I suppose that a group of ill-fed and unwashed men from distant places could play a role in transmission. Their bodies ended up in the county plot but their souls stayed at Chestnut and Kellog.

The mortal remains of others may have never left the premises. There were stories of strange deaths there, suicides and killings. As far as I know, there were never any unsolved crimes on the official records, but that was always the rumor. That's the stuff that happens when an institution in Green Bay isolates itself through foolish devotion to total sobriety. That's what can happen when the locals don't care enough to investigate the fate of missing transients.

Perhaps it's that neglect that haunted the locals. Perhaps that's why people in that time, and even in the school building for an interval, could see the comings and goings of burly phantoms of sailors. I like to think that you could redeem yourself from those hauntings by shipping out and sharing their lot. That's what I did and never saw them again. But they're seldom seen now. Like anything involving water, there's erosion and dilution. They've washed down the gutters with rain and slush right into the Fox River and out into this bay.

I shipped with a Winnebago sailor once and when he found out I was from Green Bay he said the Fox has powerful energies for those of us wedded to water. Further back than Father Marquette, further back than the Winnebago and Menominee. Back to when the waters flowed the opposite way off the glaciers. He said there was powerful stuff in a place that could go from feeding the Mississippi to feeding the St. Lawrence.

Anyway, I think that's what happens to these lake ghosts over time. The currents shift, the channels silt in here and deeper over there, and the big sand bar of your youth has disappeared entirely by your old age. So don't think that our lake ghosts are forever. They're constantly washing away. Even the phantoms of the Seaman's Ministry.

Fylgjurs of Washington Island

D oor County and Sturgeon Bay have been frequent destinations for my Wisconsin story collecting forays in the last several decades. Development has hit this area in ways that make it more difficult to hear the undistilled version of what people have experienced and how they feel about it. Ghost lore and paranormal reports both require hospitable habitats in order to thrive. The ascendance of Realtors over the settled forms of life on the land usually marks the ebbing of distinctive folkways and of lifestyles attuned to observation of the nuances of genuine sense of place.

One must go out on the tip of this peninsula if one is to find the quirky individuals who still dispense whispered hints of the strange along with the produce of roadside stands. Better yet, hop the ferry to Washington Island, which retains its traditional flavor despite development pressures of its own. While the results of my circumnavigation of the Big Sisters presents a goodly portion of relevant and cantankerous sources, Washington Island is the antidote and relief to cryptic remarks and paranoid theorizing.

My pickup truck knew exactly where to go to find Jan. He was comfortably situated in the tavern in Nelsen's Hall, the place where newcomers are served bitters as if the mix additive was a cordial. It is a good place to hear about things going on round and about Washington Island. It is where I received the tip that pointed me toward the source for the Death's Door story in "Porte des Mort's Angry Dead" in Northern Frights. *It is where I was directed to Jan's telling of the legend of Mori Thorfinnsson in "Keeper of the Northern Lights" in* Giants in the Land. *There's no end to the stories in this place or from this talkative Icelandic fisherman.*

*　　*　　*

Those of us with Icelander blood in our veins have a strong relationship to the spirits that dwell in the water and in the bowels of the Earth. I mean, have you ever been to Iceland? Ya, there's a tough speck of land in a cold inhospitable ocean. A place with a molten underbelly still cooking the land and a sea full of bobbing floes and icebergs ringing the place like sentinels. Imagine coming there in an open Viking ship a thousand years ago. Those were tough people, ones who don't scare easily, and ones who have a story to tell. Ya, Iceland makes Washington Island seem like a retreat for English country gentlemen by comparison.

Ghosts are as much a part of being Icelander as sauerkraut to a German. In old Iceland it was a mark of distinction to have a ghost or demon connected to your family. It was a way of highlighting the rigors, trials, and tribulations of the family's journeys. These were the family fylgjurs, which means follower. Fylgjurs in Iceland could be of just about any type and associated just about any activity or place. But over time they came to be connected more to life on boats, particularly in prominent families connected to heroic voyages. Those fylgjurs materialized out on the water and followed their patron's vessel.

That's how it still works around here. Though I've never seen or heard of a fylgjur beyond ten miles of Washington Island. It's as if those fylgjurs who came here to the New World got stuck right here. Ya, you gotta give them credit, this is a good place to stay.

You need a little lesson on how Icelanders of the old school see these things. The old view has spirits and magic at the center of nearly every human event and endeavor. These hauntings and unexplained events were not thought of as bad things. They just were, like the weather. Old settlements were named after supernatural events that occurred at those sites. it was accepted that most misfortune was the result of wizards tricking men into dangerous dares and foolish bets. Out on the sea it was common for these Icelanders to encounter mermen and pressure them to perform fortune telling duty. So we've had a long affiliation and affinity for things out of the ordinary.

Our Icelander ghosts come in varied forms. Plus they relate to everything around Washington Island. There are, of course, ghosts by the dozens in Porte des Mort. Many are old American Indian spirits and they seem to come in fifty-seven varieties, with tribes as far flung as the Iroquois and the Winnebago laying a claim on the place. But we have the Icelander breed out there, too, the whippers who stir up the water in a place even when it is calm elsewhere.

Then you have the surrounding specks of land, some barely big enough for a man to squat and fertilize. There was a time when the pure and undistilled Nordic ghosts feasted at Chester Thordarson's Viking Hall over on Rock Island. Now there was a man who knew how to summon the spirits from afar. Back when Thordarson ran that island as an estate there were all manner of Icelander ghosts, those of battle and sea and of the frozen wastes. The Potawatomie Light was haunted too, but that had nothing to do with Icelanders. Now that island is a park and it's more quiet. Still, the locals know that when Rock Island shuts down for the season the old ones celebrate and feast again. You can hear them on the wind.

Plum Island has a troll-like spirit that lurks in hidden places. I've spotted it once, but never had a real encounter. I'm told he can be fairly disagreeable and will sever a boat line if given half a chance.

Hog Island doesn't amount to much in square feet. It's the postage stamp of our half-apostle chain of islands. But it has some of the strangest happenings connected to it. As small as it is, sort of a magnet for washed up bodies. Two or three times for sure in real life and more often in spirit form. That is an old Icelander form of haunting, the wave-rider, where a roaming spirit of a man lost at sea will show up in distant places looking for others of his kind.

Detroit Island has the scarier type, the wailer. They're pretty much what you'd guess from a name like that. They wail out of loneliness or distress. Some say these are the ghosts of loves lost. Others called them widow ghosts, wives whose husbands never came home from the boats.

Finally you have Pilot Island with its spirit sirens. A few old knuckleheads use to say that these were like the old Greek legends or the German Lorelei. But it's a better deal than that. It's true that if you caught a glimpse and were preoccupied with watching these spirit sirens that you could smash up. The secret of these gals is that they come back on certain summer nights in their most nubile form and cavort in the buff. I'm not telling when that might be or where the best vantage point might be. I can tell you that if they catch you looking then they are transformed from youthful form to their form at death. So what was firm and perky one minute can be pretty wrinkled the next.

On Washington Island itself we have a breed of fylgjurs that follows people around from tavern to tavern. Years ago, when I was a kid, I asked my grandfather about these and wanted to know their names. He told me their names were Blatz and Pabst and I believed him for years until I repeated the names and was heartily laughed at by a group of grown men. I did find out that there were more of this type of fylgjur at one time and that they traveled as couples, one male and one female. As far as I can tell we're down to one pair now. The boy is Mori and the girl is Skotta. I've seen them straight up and still mostly possessed of my senses. But I must admit that, more often than not, they're especially seen by those whose vehicles find the ditch about 2 a.m. in the morning.

We had troublemaker ghosts years ago at the Bethel Church. Old-timers tell me that there were some wild times with hymns flying in their own and godawful smells filling the place. The best guess was that some Icelander souls just could not rest easy after a dose of the zealous evangelistic spirit of the Seaman's Friends Society that had the gospel authority over the place.

Then, too, we had the rock-flingers, but they might be more tall tale than ghost. At least I never saw one and never saw a rock arc through the air on its own. The legend here might derive from the stormy love affair between Icelanders and Washington Island farms. It took Icelanders three generations to pick the stones out of their fields. So for three generations the air was fairly whizzing with stones.

But my favorite Washington Island ghost of the old Icelander school is one I'm on good terms with. It's the rock-dweller out at Boyer's Bluff. Iceland's coast was crowded with such things. But ours is the only one of its type known in North America. He's very nimble and negotiates those high cliffs like a squirrel. The way you get this fellow to show himself is to leave him a drink somewhere. He's got bottles of beer and brandy stashed away. I leave pints of Korbel out there and before long he's humming an old ditty and having a good time. I usually am too!

Umberham's Walk

There are many back roads to explore as one drives down the peninsula toward the traditional shipbuilding centers of Sturgeon Bay and Manitowoc. This is fertile territory for ghost stories, though I found only a few that even hinted at connection to the lakes. Sturgeon Bay offered many sturdy yarns tied to the lakes. Shipbuilding there has its "John Henry" tales of strength and its fishing fleet once counted its survivors of epic lake hazards in the dozens. But there, too, no ghostly story caught the ear. The coffee shop duffers in Sturgeon Bay sent me southward. "Go to Algoma," they said.

Algoma is a friendly lakeshore community, without the bustle of Sturgeon Bay. Conversations are commenced easily there, though there's a bit more reserve than one finds on Washington Island. Tidbits of ghostly lore and short eerie accounts popped up readily in Algoma's taverns, supper clubs, and boat shops. Just not enough to make out a fleshed out narrative of meat, bones, and a three-piece suit.

The fragments armed me with enough information to zero in on the pierhead light. Which era, which light, and which lightkeeper — those were the questions that posed a jumble and tangle of oral history. Algoma possessed rich traditions relative to lighthouses and Light Service employees. There were definite clues that some of these lightkeepers made their presences felt after their mortal time allotment. Who, when, and how still proved elusive after several enjoyable hours of story swapping with harbor regulars.

Dock talk has a way of settling into vague patterns, especially when multiple sources cautiously contradict each other and incrementally embellish the central narrative. The storytellers on the docks of Algoma were far too polite to call each other liars, but their winks and arched eyebrows gave one to know that each viewed the accounts of the others as factually suspect.

Widder walked up on our assembled throng and immediately established his authority. He was one of those ramrod straight men who, despite deep face furrows and silver hair, never lose their quiet strength and moral stature. When he spoke the verbal sniping and snickering came to a halt. The sudden quiet let me know that I was about to hear the real story of the pierhead light.

*   *   *

Our light here came late in the scheme of things. We're kind of off the main lake lanes that head for Death's Door or the Soo. We missed out on the major traffic of the car ferries and freighters. It was just a matter of fishing and light package trade. But still, what with the fog we can get around here, it left the locals without an easy way to find their way home in weather thick or foul.

So in the late 1800s there was finally enough push to get a light. The first one wasn't much of a light. The old-timers called it a corn-crib with a lantern. It didn't have much height to it and so didn't have much reach. I heard it was only good for two or three miles. It cast a dark red beam that doesn't stand out very well. It was better than nothing, but just barely. And it still didn't help much in the fog.

Complaints and problems kept things evolving so that we went through several upgrades and replacements. The original light was the Ahnapee Light. That was the name of the river and the original town. The first light was at the mouth of the river and had spooky associations right from the get-go. Lightkeepers were said to see things at night and act wacky. There was an old legend about the Potawatomi having a burial ground there, but you can't put much stock in that since Indians were gone by the time things got going here. Yet there was this clear tradition.

One man in the Light Service made fun of these stories. That was Gus Umberham, a generally well thought of fellow who worked the light in the years before World War I. He was a no-nonsense kind of man who was straight and sober by lightkeeper standards. He did have one quirk, a habit of taking a boat to Kewaunee on his day off. That raised the curiosity of the locals. Was there a card game or a lady down there?

Anyway, old Gus debunked each and every report of supernatural happenings associated with the light, the harbor, and the local fishing fleet. Some thought it imprudent to be so sure of matters beyond proof. Arrogance in the face of the unknown is often a good way to invite trouble. The story handed down reported that Gus was confronted by a specter in the light tower who told him not to venture down to Kewaunee by boat anymore. Gus thought it was some seance-style trick of one of his cronies and brushed it off. He even bragged about it when he safely made the next trip down to Kewaunee.

It was the trip back that proved his undoing. The lake was a little rough that night and Umberham and his two companions paused a little before deciding they'd crossed worse. They nearly made it back to Algoma when Gus shifted his position at the same time they rolled nearly on their side through a freak wave. Over the side he went and sank with a look of panic in his eyes as if he was sucked under. This is not the first time he was pitched out of a boat nor was it the first time his boatmates were confronted with a rescue situation. Only this time there was no rescue, no bobbing, and no reaching out. He was just plain gone.

At this point it gets back to the speculation and brandy talk. There were rumors that the friends in the boat were not as close to Gus as generally thought. There was talk about hard feelings in the Light Service concerning Gus and about the desire of some to open up a position at Ahnapee Light. There was even some suggestion that another Light Service employee, Louis Braemer, exchanged harsh words with Gus. He had worked with Gus for three years and had a hard time handling Gus's opinionated nature.

Well I met Braemer as a boy, but can't claim to know the look in his eye or the grip of his hand as you'd like to in order to judge a man. Men I knew well did know him sufficiently to pronounce him not a bad sort and unlikely to indulge in homicidal urges. No, he had more the look of a privately haunted man. He did indeed confide to a few that Umberham haunted him and the light.

This was true even though the light continued to improve and evolve. It finally became the current distinctive fixture of today. They built the thousand foot concrete pier, built a higher tower of steel construction, and re-named it the Algoma Pierhead Light. It had a distinctive look due to its long elevated catwalk that permitted lightkeeper access in weather that sent the breakers over the pier. You can imagine what a walk this was when the twenty-footers were rolling on across the pier. I heard those who worked that light say that a nighttime journey across the catwalk in such a storm justified prayer and liquid fortification.

Braemer is said to have dreaded these stormy visits during the night. Who wouldn't, what with the real danger of being swept off the catwalk and smashed on the concrete? Sweet trinity, there were nights with blow enough to turn a man into a kite without the benefit of tether. Other nights brought the fog as thick as churned butter, where a lightkeeper felt suspended in the ether and could not even make out the pier below him. But it was more than weather that ate away at Braemer, more than the fickle hormones of Mother Nature. It was Umberham himself, or should I say his spirit.

Umberham, always the contrary and reckless man, chose to haunt that catwalk in the worst of times. Not content to simply make his presence known, he delighted in blocking the catwalk as if exacting tribute. The payment he required was for Braemer to brush up against him as the living lightkeeper made his way to the light. This is not a simple thing when the elements have already loosened your bowels and pumped adrenaline in your veins. Add to the mix the sight of a long dead acquaintance, rotted of countenance as a carp in a ditch, tattered, and hideous. Put the cherry on the sundae with the thought of brushing up against this grinning pile of compost and getting his whiff up your nostrils in the gale. Now multiply that experience through the twenty-odd big storms that Braemer worked in his long career.

He only ever told a few people about this experience. It wasn't that he was stoic or even particularly strong of spirit. His pure disgust precluded relating the experience to woman or child. It was not a matter for polite society, not a thing to be told to a squeamish man with a collar or doctor with the power to commit you for your own good. No, it was the type of thing that could make you feel contaminated yourself, a brush with putrification that can't be scrubbed from rain gear nor skin and certainly not the soul.

Eventually Braemer went to his reward. This made his friends think that he was finally free of his grim encounters with Umberham. That is how things should be in a just world. Some of these optimists think that Umberham now just serves lonely vigil on the catwalk in the storms. The light, like others, is no longer manned by lightkeepers. Those hopeful hearts told me that they saw the long figure of Umberham out there on the catwalk in the driving spray. But I've seen a storm or two in my time and when I looked out there in the pounding spume I saw two figures. One must be Umberham. You can take an educated guess on the identity of the other one.

Voices of the U.S.S. Cobia

There was never any doubt in my mind that this story exploration of the Upper Great Lakes would take me back to Manitowoc, Wisconsin. Over the course of many years I had developed a good many sources for tales involving the lakes and all manner of connecting transportation systems. An old labor union friend, Arthur "Tiny" Wells, had regaled me with stories of his boilermaker trade in Manitowoc's ship works long before I ever set foot in the pleasant lake city. In addition, every visit to the city's waterfront brought a pleasant encounter with friendly volunteers at the Wisconsin Maritime Museum.

Between the museum and the friendly confines of the Hamilton House, a tavern with an intoxicating bowl of lobster bisque on the menu, I heard just about every story variant relating to Lake Michigan. Rummaging around the museum always turned up fresh stories of Manitowoc's World War II role and seldom failed to provide new angles on burnished accounts of the sailing era. Visits to the Hamilton House provided endless opportunities to consort with railroaders of the car ferry era and every stripe of fisherman boater. What more can you say about a community that measures time by the arrival and departure of the S.S. Badger?

Knowing that I would end up back in Manitowoc and knowing what themes I might explore are two different things. Getting the good people of Manitowoc to talk about lake themes is never a problem. They are cheerful and mindful of their history. They stick to facts and have an eye for maritime detail. The challenge is to turn up an angle that is grim, foreboding, mysterious, or just plain wacky. Perhaps the straightforward people of Manitowoc just lacked the gene for supernatural interpretation.

On my last visit before putting this collection to bed, Ryne invited me on a Manitowoc tavern tour that turned into a visit to a number of working vessels and a rather lengthy session in the bars of Chicago Street. He was one of the few left who participated in the creation of Manitowoc's submarine fleet. There was something on his mind that he had been keeping to himself for a long time.

*   *   *

Never had much time for hocus-pocus or boogeyman stuff. Then again I never had much reason to think that it mattered one way or the other. Either that stuff exists or it doesn't, and there's probably nothing you or I can do about it. So why get worked up about it?

It's just that I'm thinking about it more and more these days. Just helped bury another pig boat man last week, a submarine construction worker. There aren't many of us left anymore. Not many who know from the cough in their lungs and the scars on their arms what exactly Manitowoc chipped in when Uncle Sam needed it. Fewer still who have any idea of the things that happened in such submarines in distant places.

There were voices in those things even as we built them. I know that must seem strange. No one ever talked about it, but occasionally I'd be working with someone, hear the shouted commands of a ship, and see that co-worker look up for the source of the voices, too. But we were under deadlines and quotas so back to work we went. No time for nonsense in wartime shipbuilding.

We built twenty-eight subs during the war. Twenty-eight fleet-equipped submarines of the Balao class came right out of the heart of the Midwest. People don't grasp the significance of this effort and this accomplishment. Imagine, building vessels three hundred feet long and almost thirty feet wide and sending them down to the Gulf of Mexico through the heart of farm country. It was an unprecedented feat in an unprecedented national emergency.

Back in the time we were working on them I thought the voices were part of the pressure to produce these subs. Maybe just the long shifts. Maybe the spirits of men lost on the deadly submarine patrols early in the war. Or maybe just the conscience of those spared military service. Most of us were unfit for military service, though a few were labeled too valuable to draft. A few of us might have been a bit guilty about that. But mostly it was a motivation to make what contribution we could here in Manitowoc. Everyone who worked on those subs knew that the crews would deal with circumstances of cramped quarters and isolation for intervals beyond the endurance of most people.

I went through the entire war without thinking much about those voices. We were under orders not to talk about our work. There were also rumors about secret communication equipment and top secret experiments. So it was a time to mind your own business and keep your mouth shut. I think on some level I thought the voices were kind of premonitions about things that would be said by crews once the subs were launched. It's funny that I would think that; it wasn't like today where almost everyone has seen a submarine movie. We didn't have any idea what was said on a submarine.

For a long time I didn't think about this at all. The last one, the *U.S.S. Mero*, was launched early 1945 and was not fully commissioned until right around the Japanese surrender. So the last one we made never saw a lick of war. Then we were done with that work.

It all flooded back to me again in 1970 when they brought the *U.S.S. Cobia* back to Manitowoc for the museum. I angled my way into passenger status on the tug *Erich*, which pulled the *Cobia* into the harbor. Right away I sensed something different in the air, like a low buzz of a bad hearing aid. That's the strange thing about hearing voices at my age, when you can barely hear at all. So it went as I found ways to hang around and help out during the preparation for the *Cobia* for public exhibition. The voices from three decades before were still there.

This time it was a bit different, more noisy than before. There were overlapping voices, with more urgency. That's when I knew that the voices I heard in the 1940s were not premonitions, they were focused commands and thoughts from submariners. The submarines themselves are like big radio receivers and recording devices. The things said underwater found their way to *Cobia* and get stored right in its metallic structure.

Everything is there from the shakedown cruises to the long sweaty patrols. There are commands to dive and to fire. There's regular radio traffic. There's laughter and the sound of fear. It seems that the *Cobia* stored not only its own sounds, but also the sounds of the other Manitowoc subs and the rest of the American sub fleet. Sometimes I think I even hear Japanese, German, and other foreign voices, but I don't know those languages.

At my age you start to wonder about these things. Do these things of our past endure? Is there a place where the young men lost in those submarines stay forever young and forever committed to the cause that claimed their lives? Are such voices a preview of the timeless well of human experience that waits for us after death? I know that you don't have answers for those questions, but those are the questions on my mind.

It's hard to tell whether this is a ghost thing or if it is more the product of human activity. Or maybe the two are intertwined in some way. I mean, the idea of spook crews on decommissioned subs is kind of absurd. Still, there's an awful lot we don't know about the effects of our actions and technologies. I happen to believe that all large human undertakings have their own energy and their own make. I think that's true from the time of King Solomon's Temple right up to the time of the Sears Towers. That goes double for destructive devices and implements of violence. Think about a nuclear warhead or an intercontinental ballistic missile. They must have impact on everything around them just by being. Then you have a submarine fleet, built on the jewel of the Great Lakes, slipping down a canal and into the Mississippi River, and then off to the ocean depths to seek out the enemy.

Next time you visit the *Cobia*, listen more closely. Whether you believe these are ghosts or just echoes in the minds of an almost gone generation doesn't matter. Whatever they are, they are reminders of a great and horrible undertaking. And when I've gone listen to hear if old shipbuilders' voices eventually join those of the crews.

Legacy of the Phoenix

Victims claimed by the Big Sisters are a diverse lot, the maritime trades being deserving of the multi-ethnic label even in the days when the various immigrant groups kept to themselves ashore. Some lines might employ more than their share of Scandinavians, certain fishing villages might trace virtually all resident bloodlines to a single Baltic port, or a particular lakefaring trade might for a period see dominance by Scots or New England Yankees. But the demographics of lakefaring are almost that of the sea, with African-American freemen and Mediterranean sailors showing up on the Great Lakes by the time of the Civil War.

Incidents involving the loss of large numbers of lives seldom hit any one group or community hard. True, the loss of a single fishing vessel in a small village of inter-related families could have devastating impact. But shipwrecks with dozens or hundreds of casualties almost always drew their ill-fated crews or passengers from many hometowns or else from cities large enough to dilute the sting.

This was the case with some of the larger Great Lakes tragedies involving excursions. It sometimes happened that particular ethnic associations or neighborhood fraternal groups might charter a lake cruise and end up with multiple deaths on the lakes. The lake annals have incidents, some horrific, involving Germans, Bohemians, and Poles. No source, however, stepped forward with a tale of spirit remembrance of such incidents.

It was among the Holland Dutch in and around Sheboygan, Wisconsin, that I picked up a decade's worth of tips about such ghostly matters involving their ancestors from the Netherlands. Like the crumbs from a cookie trail, the tips eventually brought me to Archie's woodshop in Cedar Grove, Wisconsin. There I heard a tale that not only told of a haunting, but of a deep fear of the lake and an effort to overcome it.

*   *   *

Around here there are two types of Dutch: those who love the water and those who prefer terra firma. I'm in the latter category, but you can see by my current project that I'm trying to change.

Such attitudes get drummed into us as children and then you must work like the dickens to overcome them. If a couple of misfortunes pile on the original legacy, like a cousin drowning during childhood, then the whole pile of bad feelings is just reinforced.

In our case the attitudes were handed down from Grandpa Asa, as strict a Dutch Reformed layman as you'd find on the west shore of Lake Michigan. Despite his straight-laced theology, or maybe because of it, he was a big believer in ghosts and demons. This went double if the topic was the tragic *Phoenix*, the Dutch apocalypse for the area. He was convinced that our family was haunted by the ghost of the *Phoenix* and that we best stay away from the lake.

The basic story is well known around here. The *Phoenix* was carrying a shipload of immigrants from the Netherlands, over two hundred of them. It was the Autumn of 1847 and Wisconsin was not even a state. The ship caught fire off Sheboygan and only a handful of immigrants survived. The survivors settled here in Cedar Grove and dealt with the psychological aftermath. That meant everything from washed up bodies to the inquires of relatives in Holland. Grandpa Asa said they were haunted from the day they reached dry land. As evidence of this instant fate he points to a follow-up visit by the representatives of another large group of potential Dutch immigrants who considered joining them. Apparently those here were adjudged accursed and the immigrants diverted to Michigan instead.

That started the push-pull, love-hate with the lake here in Cedar Grove. Dutch around here have alternately shunned the lake or gone back to it. I guess in every generation since there has been this split and in every generation someone else was claimed by the lake. Among the Lake Michigan Dutch it is often said that there is not a lakeside Reformed Church that does not have an entry in its records for someone who didn't come back from the lake. Grandpa Asa said that here in Cedar Grove we got the worst of it, with over two hundred souls haunting us. He said he once pushed a friend into the water at night and then saw two hundred sets of accusing eyes staring at him from out on the water. Another time he saw all two hundred plus ghosts, dripping and haggard, troop up to the cemetery.

I never saw anything that dramatic. Mostly the things I saw were when I was a boy and was tempted to join friends in a boat. Any time the mere thought entered my mind I'd see children's bodies floating in the lake or clinging to driftwood. It really stuck with me. That's what this boat is about.

I realize it's a dinky thing, but not a dingy. No it's a classic flat-bottomed skiff. Yes, more a thing for ponds or sluggish creeks. I'm working up to something more adventurous. Shoot, if I get this in the water who knows what I might build next? A Frisco Bay pelican, a twenty-five foot cutter, or maybe throw an old truck engine into a scow? Well, I better not get ahead of myself.

So far I got the skiff building frame, the molds at their positions, and the transom and stems together. Next I'll notch for the chines, plank the bottom, and lay on the garboard. After that comes planing, application of the bedding compound, and laying the second bottom layer. Finally, I'll put on the rest of the planks, lap nail them, and apply the finish. That's what it takes to make a wooden boat the old way.

Lake Michigan Dutch know how to do these things, it's in the blood. The same blood that kept some fishing for generations. The same blood that took some on ships of the Goodrich Transportation Company, like the *Sheboygan*, the *Seabird*, and the *Alpena*. We lost family again when the *Seabird* went down with seventy-two souls near Waukegan after the Civil War. Then another when the *Alpena* just plain disappeared somewhere in the southern half of Lake Michigan. In 1929, we had cousins who manned the Sheboygan tugs that rescued survivors from the sunken *Senator* and another who went down on the *Wisconsin* off Kenosha. I could go on, but you get the picture.

Grandpa Asa always said that those ones who were lost on the lake were jealous of those who stayed on land. Jealous of our dry houses and warm beds, our gardens and orchards, and of our old-age and grandchildren. He believed that every one of those who went down on the *Phoenix* and everyone lost since begrudged us the comforts and rewards of life.

I don't know about that. It's true that the Dutch can be a grim lot and sometimes forget to balance life with pleasure. But as I try to find my own balance I think those ghosts are just cautions and expressions of hope. After all, we built here what those immigrants dreamed about. Why wouldn't they feel some longing for it? But I no longer believe Grandpa Asa, there's no ghostly urge to rip away our comforts or drag us down to the depths.

For myself and those like me, the ones indoctrinated with fear, there needs to be a reckoning with this legacy. We need to move past it. We need to recapture the exuberance of the Dutch that sailed the seas and built a trade empire hundreds of years ago. There's no life without risk, no possibility of gain without the potential for loss.

The fact that even those of us with morbid fears of the lake stayed near it is evidence of the pull of it on our souls. If we were meant to be elsewhere we would have moved to Montana by now. But you realize as you get older that those of us susceptible to being haunted would be haunted anywhere. No matter what your heritage, there's always a skiff to be built and a *Phoenix* to be put to rest.

Light Station Storyteller

I t's not often that those of us who collect, write, and tell stories become the focus of subsequent lore. For every Washington Irving or Mark Twain enshrined in our consciousness of the North American narrative, there are thousands upon thousands of more modest voices who have kept local peculiarities alive in both the archival and oral tradition sense. What would be left of our sense of place and our understanding of local culture had not those feeling an affinity for vanishing folkways either written down or retold these local tales?

The issue becomes dicier when applied to those who record or retell stories of the supernatural. Those of us in this trade know full well that we run the risk of being thought crackpots or eccentrics, no matter how balanced our treatment of the material. It is true that some story weavers are characters in their own right and magnets for all types of bizarre encounters. But it is equally true that a larger number of preservers of strange oral accounts live rather humdrum lives, marked only by one or two atypical events that open their mental portals to the possibility of still stranger things.

Perhaps those of us who dig up and reassemble story shards don't recognize that the central characters in those accounts might have been storytellers themselves. Perhaps that's what makes the story resonate down to the present. Perhaps that's what keeps the spirit of the narrative in vital condition. The ability of a storyteller to project this resonance and vitality from beyond the grave might be a type of haunting. Maybe we just miss that part of the dynamic in our fascination with things macabre or eerie.

This story collector almost missed the possibility of such a dynamic in stories in and around Port Washington, Wisconsin. In more than a half-dozen trips to the community first called Wisconsin City when it was founded in 1835, I had gleaned material on the Lewis family and their connection to the Old Port Washington Light Station. But that biographical segment of local maritime lore did not have an obvious connection to my bulging folder on phantoms, apparitions, and sundry spirits connected to this old port.

*Ward straightened me out on that account during a walk on the break-
water path. He confessed status as a "remote relative" of the old Lewis
clan. What's more, he made a strong case that storytelling is at the core of
haunting and the storytellers can become the most vigorous of ghosts.*

*   *   *

The spinning of yarns, the nose for the strange, and the ability to
attract the unusual were genetic traits in the Lewis family. They
became legends, but first themselves told legends. It think this is
what some call "living mythically." In other words, knowing what
sets of values and heroism will appeal to people and then applying
it in a magnified way to one's own actions and the accounts one
tells about others. This is why we have the term "larger than life"
for circumstances where the sum of the experience is greater than
that of the parts of individual actions. We call these things legends,
extraordinary events, or paranormal powers depending upon how
they appear to us.

Anyhow, the Lewis family knew how to exist mythically, right
down to their sense of timing and how to live. The family patriarch
was Captain Charles Lewis and the title was not a trumped up hon-
orific. He had logged a long career as a captain of whaling vessels
out of New England and later packets on the Great Lakes. He comes
into the Port Washington picture in a semi-retirement that installs
him as a lightkeeper at the light station on the bluff. The year was
1874 and the sturdy light station was a scant fourteen years old.

This station was already a legend. It replaced a nearby 1840s
light tower that was practically an ancient world artifact on the
order of a hilltop bonfire. The light station brought an oil-fueled
fresnel lens that could pierce twenty miles into the darkness. The
station itself looked more like a church than a lighthouse. It already had its share of characters, stories, and chilling incidents by
the time of Captain Lewis's arrival. He immediately took the place
over and conducted it with flair.

One of the ways he instantly made his mark was by the perpetu-
ation of colorful and off-beat accounts about the previous
lightkeeper, a fellow named Hoyt. The Captain used the moniker
"Hoyt of the Night," in a play on words suggesting the height and
darkness of the light tower setting. He regaled children with stories of Hoyt's fondness for liver and suggested that washed up bodies were often missing livers. Later he maintained that Hoyt's ghost
haunted he light station and the bluff.

What's curious about this part of the captain's repertoire is the likelihood that the captain initially pulled these Hoyt stories out of thin air. Then later he confided to family members that he was indeed having encounters with Hoyt's ghost. Isn't that something? Makes you wonder about the power of an idea to shape experience. That, or else the impact of accidental conjuring up of the dead through reckless claims.

Anyway, the captain became well-established in this vein and was expected to pontificate on just about any abnormal occurrence or tragedy involving the lake or men on it. This could be any subject from weather shifts, to vessels gone missing, to where fish might be found. With the captain such discussions took the listener on a global tour. An answer about the oft-damaged Port Washington pier might involve references to icebergs in the North Atlantic and reefs in the South Pacific. If the listener was extremely well-liked the reply might even include detours into time spent with headhunters and the discovery of a friend's tatooed arm in a shark's gullet. That and remarks about the spirits of dozens of departed former shipmates who visited the captain in the night.

He cut quite a figure in his whaler's coats, armed with spyglass, and pennants flying, while patrolling the widow's walk of the old light station. He would have been still talked about a hundred and twenty years after his death even if he hadn't stayed to haunt the place. But maybe it was what his son said about him that turned storyteller into haunting spirit.

If anything, son Charles, Jr. was an even more gifted storyteller. While the captain got by on the romance of his life's experiences and the combination of gruff demeanor and a twinkle in the eye, the son had a genuine flair for theatrics. After the captain's death his wife served as lightkeeper for a sort interval. Then Charles, Jr. took over for a forty-four year stint that was loaded with drama and heroics. Brought up on the accounts of his father's exploits, he was not about to go quietly into the night of lightkeeping. He was involved in an inordinate amount of lifesaving situations for a lightkeeper. He braved rough lake conditions many times in open boats and sometimes swam to the rescue. He was viewed as a shining example of virility and manliness.

Charles, Jr. also took it as his personal mission to enlarge and preserve his father's legacy and legend. During his long tenure he related light station and harbor lore to three separate generations of Port Washington youngsters. He spared no effort to put Captain

Lewis square in the middle of this story pantheon.

Not that he had to try hard, especially after the captain made his debut as a light station specter. Charles, Jr. accepted that development in stride as the natural culmination of his father's extraordinary career. He even had rationales for the captain's transition to haunting presence. There was, after all, plenty of travel to distant lands with exotic spiritual habits. This meant the captain had been exposed to voodoo, Borneo curses, and Siberian magic. Add to these strange experiences a long career of rivalries and professional jealousies and one could find those with motive to send bad karma the Captain's way. Charles, Jr. put this all forth as a theory why the Captain remained tethered to the light station.

That's all well and good, but how about the possibility that an old thespian, despite death, remained reluctant to leave the stage? The Lewis family loved to ham it up. The captain was definitely one to abandon Paradise and haunt earthly spots if it meant a rapt audience. His son's constant invoking of his name and memory must have had the lure of a studio applause sign.

Well, those are the main parts of the explanation about how the Lewis clan came to occupy such a large niche in Port Washington legends. But can you call the accounts exaggerations? I don't think so. Everything that I could find about them in the way of recorded fact was extraordinary. I was not surprised at all when I found an old-timer who swore he was saved from drowning twice as a child by Charles, Jr., once while the lightkeeper was still living and once after his death. That these men would become ghosts is just about the least surprising thing about them.

So I'll tell you to do what I tell everybody else. Wait for late summer or an early autumn evening with a nice moon. Head up the bluff to where the local historical society has restored the light station building. If you can tell me afterwards that you didn't see, hear, or feel anything, well, then I'd say stick to accounting or tax preparation. Story ciphering and ghost hunting aren't your cup of tea.

Milwaukee's Coast Guard Ghosts

T he official guardians of coastal and inland waters have been alluded to in several stories in this collection. The U.S. Coast Guard has a record of distinguished service to mariners and pleasure boaters. This record includes many rescues, fatal rescue attempts, and involvement in inexplicable events. Charting such events is a bit complicated by the evolution of the Coast Guard and some of its predecessor agencies. Light station service and shore-line life saving service was eventually folded into the customs and maritime rescue functions of the Coast Guard proper. Few federal operations have bounced around between so many departments, while the bureaucracy redefined the mission from revenue to commerce to transportation, and, in time of war, to naval defense.

Government agencies are singularly unhelpful at identifying unusual activity that occurs within their jurisdictions, and the Coast Guard is no exception. Hundreds, if not thousands, of official reports have logged unusual sightings and out of the ordinary events. The oral tradition of Coast Guardsmen is filled with the bizarre, the chilling, and the curious. Yet there is almost no agency interest in compiling or analyzing such information.

It is not easy to get individual members, officers or enlisted, to talk about these things. Many requests for leads on such matters produced zero referrals. The final options were to glean the cryptic logs and reconstruct incidents or to abandon the Coast Guard perspective entirely.

An invitation from Milwaukee friends to spend a day salmon fishing brought a breakthrough. My friends provided some exceptional professional services to a fellow who had a fine boat down in Milwaukee's McKinley Marina. The grateful client turned out to be Wilson, a retired career Coast Guardsman. He was adamant about the strange powers derived from flirting with life and death on Lake Michigan.

*   *   *

If I learned anything at all in my years on cutters on the ocean and open boats on the lakes, it's that saving a life is no guarantee of immortality for yourself. Or even peace of mind. Men who spend their lives on the water looking after others develop some special attitudes with some special burdens. I learned that right off the bat here in Milwaukee. Early in my service time I was stationed at the Milwaukee Breakwater Lighthouse.

Let me tell you, lighthouse tending was not among the favored assignments among the "coasties." Most that I knew would take iceberg patrol or Aleutian Island airfield duty over lighthouse duty. When the Coast Guard took over the lighthouse network it automated most of the small ones on land, the mom and pop lights. What it kept for service personnel were the big lights that were cut off from things or sitting out in places that bore the brunt of storms. Milwaukee's Breakwater Lighthouse was one such place.

We came and went in a twenty-five open lifeboat, in weather you wouldn't believe. We had three days on and three days off. Three days of sleep deprivation with two or three other bug-eyed enlisted men. You couldn't sleep in that concrete coffin with its million decibel foghorn. In addition they had us busy with all sorts of chores that the old time lightkeepers never had to worry about.

Where the Coast Guard manned lighthouses there were weather observations to take, radio traffic to monitor, buoys to tend, lights to replace at other towers, and all sorts of maintenance to perform in godawful weather. We didn't get to sit and read books or watercolor like so many people think. And when we got cut off by a storm, with no relief crew in sight, it seemed like the world itself was ending. Believe it or not, that big concrete block, which looks like it could take a direct nuclear hit, shook with the waves we took out there. That's when you took stock of who you were and where you'd been.

It's times like that that leave some of us coasties with the ability to see things that others miss. Things like weather signs, changes in how birds are acting, and just the instinct to know something terribly wrong or incredibly goofy was about to happen. Call it a sixth sense or whatever, but a good storm tune-up and resulting scare was just the ticket to let you know when the boneheads of Lake Michigan might put themselves and others in danger. Not that you knew while the waves were pounding the lighthouse. No, during those times it was playing cards and telling dirty jokes, like whistling past the cemetery. It was later, sometimes much later, often on a beautiful day when the bad thoughts would just jump up and bite you in the ass.

Coasties who developed those instincts could see forwards and backwards. Yessir, a storm-rattled brain gets rewired to glimpse the future and the past. Now this might be ghosts or it might be more of the level of ESP. One old Chief[7] I knew came down on the side of ghosts. Or as he put it, "Ghosts what were and ghosts-to-be." He might have been right about that, you've seen the haunted looks on those destined for untimely ends.

In any event, there was more of that sort of thing at the Milwaukee Breakwater Lighthouse than just about anywhere I've been. More than Cape Hatteras, Key West, and Puget Sound put together. Why? Hell if I know. Old sailor's curse, Potawatomi magic, the departure of the Braves for Atlanta, or Bud Selig's flush of all of baseball down into the holding tank? There's no reason for things like that in the end. It's just the way things are.

All I know is that there was nothing like a big storm at the lighthouse to get someone out there to think that the old *Milwaukee* car ferry had just steamed by. Even though every bit of Great Lakes lore informed us it was permanent fish habitat way out in the lake. Others would see the limping *Marquette*, the ship that hit and sank the *Senator*. Sometimes it might be a matter of seeing lakecraft from boaters or fishermen in one storm getting a distress call from those craft in the next storm, and then seeing those craft in a third storm after they went missing for good.

Some of this Milwaukee tendency for seeing ghost ships, ghost mariners, and other Lake Michigan oddities goes back a ways in time. Stories in the lighthouse talked about pioneer times, canoes, and fur traders. But that's pretty thin chowder for this coastie. I'll vouch for something not quite that far back, a thing I heard from the bosun's mouth as it were. That was the tradition that came down from *U.S. Lightship 95*, the vessel that set off Milwaukee closer to the main ship lanes.

Experiences out on *Lightship 95* made our breakwater light experiences look like marshmallow roasts at Cub Scout camp. They were really out in the thick of it. You hear things like forty-foot seas and near misses by ore boats and being battered by timbers swept off sunken ships. Like the old bosun said, "experiences that put hair on your chest, gray your beard, and make the hair in your skivvies fall out.

They, too, saw the *Milwaukee* out on *Lightship 95* before it sank and afterward. As far as I know, the lightship crew made the last reliable sighting of the *Milwaukee* on its final voyage. But then they saw it pretty much every year until old 95 was taken away. I've even heard that *Lightship 95* was haunted by the *Milwaukee's* skipper, Captain "Heavy Weather" McKay. Guess the old fellow took residence in the lightship til the end.

The old bosun said the lightship crews saw the ghosts of many of the mid-lake wrecks and other maritime disasters that involved the Port of Milwaukee in some way. He said the ill-fated *Chicora* was a frequent visitor, even thought it went down way back in 1894. But he added that it was common on the lightship to see the hulks and timbers of all sorts of unknown lake casualties.

Some young whippersnappers ask me why we saw those things back then and Coast Guardsmen don't see such things today. Hell, nobody sees anything, feels anything today. They're all removed from experience, all got their heads stuck up a computer's ass. Hell, there's GPS, radar, satellite imagery, and weather fax! Who the hell even looks at the lake?

This has happened to every lake trade as things got automated and mechanized. The old bosun told me that it started back when steam replaced sail. That's when the trend away from the connection of able-bodied sailor, vessel, heaven, and water began. With sail there was a direct tie to the elements and desperate need for all hands in times of distress. Engines put men below deck, gave them engineering titles, and more specialization followed. So it came to be that not all on the water shared the same experience. But we sure did on the breakwater lighthouse.

So over time not everyone on the water saw things the same way or reported what they saw the same way. That makes these old Lake Michigan stories a dying breed of talk. Same with the Coast Guard stories. This is not just a breakdown of our common lake heritage. Hell no, it's a breakdown of etiquette and common courtesy. In my day the loss of a vessel was a horrible thing and it called for reverent and dignified treatment, even it if caused people to see odd things. Now a lakecraft loss is more an opportunity for rubberneckers and commentators. Look at the circus the loss of the *Linda E*[8] set off. There were goofs who came into that deal who did everything but claim UFO abduction, the boat's on the grassy knoll in Dallas, and that there's a Coast Guard conspiracy.

Maybe there is a Lake Michigan triangle like Bermuda's. Maybe there's more to all of this than old coasties are likely to know. But I do know a thing or two. I know that those spirits of the lake saw us as kin at one time and knew we had spunk enough that showing themselves was not likely to soil our skivvies.

A Boyhood Memory of the Wreck of the Wisconsin

The first story in this collection credits a former naval aviator with provoking the curiosity that in turn generated this book. It was not as if no lake stories had come my way prior to that chance meeting in O'Hare Airport. My travels had taken me to many harbor towns, and I had found most blessed with maritime legends and lore.

What was less certain before my O'Hare encounter was whether there was enough material to fill a book-length collection. Readers who have completed this circumnavigation in print can judge whether the stories connect with their sense of the Upper Great Lakes and whether I've presented the material to their liking. But I doubt few will quarrel with my conclusion that there are, indeed, generous quantities of strange things on these lakes that merit inquiry and retelling.

Just as it is appropriate to begin the book with the tale that inspired the collection, it is only fair to end the book with the first personal account of a lake tragedy that I encountered in my travels. As with so many stories and clues I have collected, it was not easy to know what exactly was represented by the account. Hindsight permits the interpretation of youthful trauma and its lingering aftermath. At the time of the telling I thought the account spoke only to the psychological impact of the event. Revisiting this account again, with its Kenosha source, Kenton, dead over a decade, allows me to understand how one child was haunted by lake ghosts and passed it on to others.

* * *

Lots of lake memories in my family. Our ancestors came here in the 1820s off of Lake Erie, when the place was called Pike. It was a wild place then, with a few boatmen supplying a handful of homesteaders. The family legend has it that one of our forebears created the first light on the west side of Lake Michigan by finding a huge prairie white oak near shore, cutting it off twelve or fifteen feet up, and burning fires on this immense stump.

In the beginning the lake trade ran mostly to Chicago and over to Michigan. When Milwaukee built up, our harbor became Southport, the main stop on the early Chicago to Milwaukee packets. Our people were part of that and were well-established in the shipping and fishing trades.

It was my uncle's fishing boat that kept me close to Kenosha harbor. My father had died of influenza right after I was born, so I grew up mostly under my uncle's supervision. He had lots of chores for me around the boat and I was already pulling my weight by the time I was 10 or 11 years old. Anyway, that's the reason I was at the dock shack early that October morning in foul weather.

This was 1929, you know, and the *Milwaukee* had just gone down the week before. It was season of bad weather, but everybody expected that it would break soon and we would be out again before winter. A big tragedy like the one of the week before gets everyone around a harbor edgy. There had been false alarms of other ships running aground and a few out of Kenosha that had to be towed in. So when we heard harbor commotion that morning we thought it was in that vein. We didn't realize the Coast Guard was going out. Then at first light crowds started to come down to the piers. We looked out toward the lake and saw a ship just about on its side about a mile out.

It was the *Wisconsin*, but we didn't know that at the time. We stood there for a minute and my uncle patted me gently on the head. It was a tender gesture for a rough man, but it told me he was sorry about the knuckle rap he applied to my skull a few days before. You see, I had a dream that a ship would go down off Kenosha and that I would see a blue-faced captain's body wrapped in a tarp. My uncle attributed my dream to hysteria and the recent loss of the *Milwaukee*. I got the knuckles on my head when I insisted the ship was not a car ferry and was off Kenosha.

Soon it was clear to my uncle that there were men to be rescued out there. So he hollered to men who came to watch the disaster and got about six on his boat to help out. He didn't know that I found my way onboard, he kept me off in heavy weather, but I wasn't about to miss out on this trip. I held a light while they started the engines and no one questioned my presence. Soon we were under way and cut past the piers where waves were running as big as I've ever seen them.

When we got out to the wreck it was a scene from hell. I remember trembling and feeling queasy. Men in the water were screaming, thrashing at the water, and some were tangled in lines or unable to get out of sloshing piles of debris thrown around by the waves. There was so much junk in the water banging into my uncle's boat that it made it hard to get to the drowning men. We actually looked into the faces of some who were exhausted and gave their final screams and then sank out of sight. Those are things that stay with you the rest of your life.

We picked up a lot of men, at least twenty. It could have been more. And some bodies. I remember how happy we were that we had saved so many. But on the way back in we actually had more who died from exposure. We just couldn't get them all warm quick enough. It sure soured the mood on that boat. For awhile we didn't think we'd get any of them in alive.

I remember how somber the men were when they carried the bodies off the boat. Quite a crowd had gathered by then and you had the usual strange behavior that one finds at tragedies. I remember a young woman pulling a button off a victim's coat. But the thing I remember most is the body they brought off in a tarp. It was Captain Morrison, and he was blue-faced just like in my dream.

Over the weeks and months to come I would learn more about Captain Morrison. Crewmen who were treated in Kenosha hospitals said he was a good man and had done what he could to save the ship. There was the irony that he was good friends with the lost captain of the *Milwaukee*. Public discussion established that he had been a generally prudent ship's master.

There was quite a big deal in Kenosha for a long time because of the wreck of the *Wisconsin*. There were boards of inquiry and a coroner's inquest that picked at every scab of the tragedy. The newspapers printed sensational headlines with very little to back them up. Some of the scandalmongers picked on Captain Morrison, who was unavailable to defend himself. Some said he should have beached his ship, others said he should have made for the piers. I don't know the whole story or who's right. But I can say that it was rough out there and it seems like the ship went down too fast to do much of anything.

Others picked on the Coast Guard, second-guessing the rescue effort. Kenosha's Coast Guard only had small boats and could only take on so many survivors. They took on the ones who had abandoned ship before all the debris complicated the situation. The *Wis-*

consin was still half-afloat at the point and only half the crew was off her. They made a second trip out, but by that time the Coast Guard's boats were no match for the swells of cargo.

I'm not ashamed to say that the whole event stuck with me in a really emotional way. It was my first close-up brush with death. It was also my first realization of the power of the lake and how it could kill. You don't forget that, especially when that captain in a tarp comes back to you now and then. Just in fleeting ways, a glimpse of his body in the bottom of a rowboat or a brief flash of his blue face in the water.

At first I thought I was crazy. You know, kind of shell-shocked to see such things as a kid. But over the years I met others from that time who admitted that they saw things that looked like the dead from the *Wisconsin*. One time we were on a family fishing outing and an empty oarboat drifted by us. We lined it in thinking someone had lost it and we would turn it in. When I reached out to steady it I was jolted by the brief appearance of Captain Morrison, blue face and all. I said nothing, but later my grandson asked me, "Grandpa, was there a man with a funny colored face in that boat?" What a relief! I didn't feel alone anymore.

At that moment the comforting words of my uncle finally made sense. When I had asked him after the wreck of the *Wisconsin* whether its dead crew had suffered he was a bit slow to respond. He thought a bit and said, "Perhaps a moment or two, but then they just eased into that comforting bath of those who have gone missing."

Footnotes

[1] the term used by the Chippewa/Ojibwe peoples to describe the collective of all their related bands.

[2] Reservation cars

[3] Anishinabe Medicine Society

[4] ancestral prophecies of the Anishinabe

[5] the leader of the lodge

[6] apprentices

[7] chief petty officer

[8] a commercial fishing boat lost in 1998